Decoys and Aggression

A Police K9 Training Manual

Stephen A. Mackenzie

Detselig Enterprises Ltd.
Calgary, Alberta

Canadian Cataloguing in Publication

Mackenzie, Stephen A. (Stephen Alexander), 1948-
  Decoys and aggression

  ISBN 1-55059-132-0

  1. Police dogs – Training. 2. Police dogs – Training – Study and
teaching. 3. Dogs – Training. 4. Dogs – Training – Study and
teaching. I. Title.
HV8025.M32 1996   636.7'0886   C96-910156-2

Detselig Enterprises Ltd.
1220 Kensington Road NW, Unit 210
Calgary, Alberta T2N 3P5

Distributed by:

Temeron Books Inc.
P.O. Box 896
Bellingham, Washington 98227

Temeron Books Inc.
1220 Kensington Road NW, Unit 210
Calgary, Alberta T2N 3P5

Printed in Canada   SAN 115-0324   ISBN 1-55059-132-0

Contents

Figures

All photos in Chapter 6 by Darryl Lindsay

All photos in Chapter 7 by Darryl Lindsay

. . . .

Detselig Enterprises Ltd. expresses its appreciation for the financial assistance for its 1996 publishing program from Canadian Heritage and The Alberta Foundation for the Arts, a beneficiary of the Lottery Fund of the Government of Alberta.

COMMITTED   ALBERTA
TO THE   Lotteries
DEVELOPMENT   The Alberta
OF CULTURE   Foundation
AND   for the Arts
THE ARTS   Alberta

1

The Role of the Decoy

At some point in protection and apprehension training, someone has to lure the dog into thinking they are behaving so badly they deserve to be bitten. This person has had many titles over the years. When I first started decoying back in the late seventies, I was known as an agitator, since I jumped around a lot and generally got the dog all excited. Then I found that some people referred to me as a catcher, since the end result of my efforts was to catch the dog on a protective sleeve. Later, when I started working with sport trainers they called me a helper, since my job was to help the dog learn and perfect its skills. Apparently many of them felt the terms agitator and catcher were inadequate to describe the scope of the work done.

The older terms seemed to suggest that all you had to do was to jump around, annoy the dog and take a bite from it in order to do your job well. The scope of the helper's work is indeed far beyond that. At some point in the process someone called me a "decoy," since I was luring the dog into the belief that I was either a bad person, a violent criminal or at least someone who needed biting from time to time. This term has proven to be my favorite since the decoy not only helps the dog learn, but often uses role deception. When meeting trained dogs for the first time, a valuable use of the decoy is not in regular drills but in dress rehearsals, where the dog thinks the threat is real and the decoy is still a stranger. Recently I have heard the term "quarry" used, particularly by trainers from the western United States and Canada. It is a good term, but my favorite is still "decoy." For simplicity, this book will use the term decoy, but feel free to substitute whatever word you prefer.

A Valuable Tool

A good decoy is a K-9 trainer's most valuable tool. When it comes to aggression work, a good decoy will have a very positive influence on the dogs being trained. The decoy can take a poor dog and make it mediocre, a mediocre dog and make it good, or can take a good dog and make it excellent. On the other hand, a poor decoy can have devastating effects. An excellent dog will become mediocre or worse, as will a good dog. A dog that was mediocre to begin with has no chance at all with a bad decoy – it will be completely ruined. In some cases poor decoys have completely ruined even good dogs. So the decoy must not only have skill but must be a disciplined person committed to working cooperatively with the trainer. The purpose is to provide the trainer with a human being that behaves exactly as the trainer needs at any given time during the dog's development. Consequently the decoy must be able to act in different manners and change style quickly. In many instances the actions of the decoy are actually in control of the training and learning process and there is a tendency for the decoy to think that he or she is more than just a tool. This is a trap that all good decoys resist since there can only be one trainer on the field at a time for best results. Many trainers, having trouble finding good decoys, and having no desire to argue with them once they get big heads, learn to decoy themselves. They realize that if something is really important, they must be able to do it themselves in order to control the training process.

A Communication Expert

The good decoy is an expert in canine communication, understands what the dog is saying at all times and understands what actions are appropriate to fit the trainer's overall plan for the dog. To do this the decoy begins by studying the paralanguage of the dog until able to read dogs well. Once this is mastered, the decoy must learn how to speak back to the dog using the same body gestures and behaviors that dogs use to communicate with each other.

An Aggression Manipulator

Once competent as a communication expert, the decoy needs to understand the natural forms of aggression in dogs and what behaviors and language will trigger each individual type. Only then is he or she able to trigger the particular form of aggression the trainer desires at the correct time and avoid triggering aggression when the trainer is trying to do control work.

That, in a nutshell, describes the good decoy – reads dogs well – is in excellent shape physically and skillful enough to speak the dog's language – knowledgeable enough to use that physical skill to trigger or develop different forms of aggression at the proper times and can avoid stimulating aggression when it is not appropriate.

Decoying is a precise skill that requires physical ability and mental discipline. If you desire to prove your courage or are trying to impress people, please stay away from decoying. Eventually you will do something foolish and get hurt, but worse than that, you will hurt a dog, either physically or mentally. If you need to prove yourself, there are activities such as bungee jumping and sky diving, etc. Take up one of those and do us all a favor by leaving dogs alone.

2

Physical Requirements

It is true that almost anyone can put on a sleeve and take a bite, but few people become good decoys. Being a decoy is an extremely physical game, as well as a mental one. It is actually an athletic contest, and you are competing with a world class athlete (the dog). If you are not in the peak of physical condition, do not expect to excel in this field. I repeatedly see people twenty pounds overweight, or breathing heavily due to cigarette use, or just plain weak from being out of shape, trying to decoy. They can let the dog bite them alright, but the dog never gets what it really needs.

When people prepare themselves for the other phases of dog training, such as aggression control or tracking, they first ensure that they have the proper equipment. This is wise. They would never start an aggression control lesson without their leash, or a tracking session without certain equipment such as leads, collars or harnesses, depending on the style of tracking they have chosen. They know that it is foolish to begin dog work without the correct equipment. And yet they think they can begin decoy work without a good body. This is a fallacy. The most important equipment for decoy work is a knowledgeable mind inside a good, sound body that can stand up to anaerobic and aerobic stresses, has good upper body strength, a good sense of timing, balance, quick reactions, coordination, a strong, healthy back and the ability to absorb pain occasionally. If you would not do control work without the correct equipment, you should not do decoy work without it either.

Which brings us to the difficult part of the story. The above listed qualities are essentially God given gifts. They are encoded in the genetic material of each individual. It is sometimes painful but nonetheless important to realize that some people have these gifts and others do not. For those who have the genetic potential, hard work will hone their skills and improve their abilities immensely. However, people who do not have the genetic programming for items such as physical coordination and quickness can work hard for the rest of their lives and never improve enough to become good decoys. Fortunately, everyone has a gift for something, and these people should move on to what they are programmed for in order to have happy, fulfilling lives. They should not frustrate themselves trying to do something at which they will never excel.

Before beginning decoy training, it is important to have your physician check you out. If you are not in good general health the extra stress of decoying could be detrimental. Once you have the "go ahead" from your doctor, the next step is to get into shape. This, of course, is a real can of worms since there are many ways to do so. Several methods I have seen people employing are dangerous and unnecessary, so be careful how you approach this topic. There is no quick fix for being out of shape, so be prepared to spend some time getting into shape slowly and carefully. If you have a method of choice which is approved by your physician, by all means stick with it. If you don't, you may want to start by reading the *ACSM Fitness Book* by the American College of Sports Medicine. Published by Leisure Press of Champaign, IL (ISBN 0-88011-460-6) it describes a method of evaluating your present state of fitness and then suggests a responsible approach to improving it. You could also consult one of the many fitness professionals in your area.

Whatever way you do it, make sure that you have the proper equipment before you start decoying. It is a physical competition and you simply have to be in good shape to succeed.

One last, but important thought. There comes a time in the career of all decoys when they need to stop decoying. Whether it is due to age, failing health or injury, they all lose the ability to decoy effectively at some point. The dogs get faster, the equipment heavier and decoys look for techniques which require less running. They have better judgment, but are best used in an advisory capacity from then on.

It is difficult for any athlete to recognize when it is time to retire, and decoys are no exception. However, it is important for them to do so. When the time comes, stop decoying. It is better for you, better for the trainer, and better for the dogs.

3

Canine Communication

Once you have established the physical requirements, the next task is to study the language of the dog. If the confidence level of a dog changes in the middle of a drill, the decoy must be able to read this instantly, knowing exactly what the trainer wants done should this happen. If the decoy understands what the dog is saying at all times and reacts the way a good trainer has indicated, many problems in aggression training can be avoided. Problems which already exist can be alleviated also. Without this ability to read the dog, a decoy is much less valuable, and in some cases a hindrance. Any way you look at it, a decoy must master the language of the dog in order to be useful.

Dogs communicate in several ways. Probably the best known form is auditory (with sound). Few people have been around dogs for any length of time without hearing one bark, growl, whine or howl. All of these have some function, although humans do not understand them completely.

Auditory

The whine serves as a plea for assistance. This soft, high pitched sound is first used when the animal is a puppy to obtain assistance from the bitch (a technical term for the mother of a dog). This function seems to remain throughout life, so that even adult dogs whine when they are seeking help. The growl is usually a form of threat or warning. It is often the precursor to aggression and as such can be a sign that the dog is unhappy with something and is considering doing something violent to solve its problems. The bark is a sign of excitement. The fact that many stray dogs do not bark suggests to some people that the bark may have something to do with marking or defending territory or personal space. The howl seems to serve as a long distance marker, so that packs can avoid each other's territory.

Olfactory

Dogs also communicate through their olfactory senses (their sense of smell). They often mark their territory through urinating on the boundaries so that other dogs will smell their markers and know enough to stay out. It is suspected that from the smell of urine a dog can tell which individual dog marked the spot. There are recorded instances where humans have kept wild wolves out of their camp by urinating around the site in canine fashion. Males can certainly tell if the urine is from a female ready to breed. Dogs will also use the front end of their tongues to force air samples through a small hole between the gums and the upper lip. This sends the air sample back above the soft palate to the vomeronasal organ which gives them a better idea of what chemicals are in the air.

Tactile

A certain amount of communication occurs through the tactile sense (the sense of touch). The bitch has to lick neonatal puppies (puppies less than three weeks old) in order to stimulate them to urinate and defecate. Licking is also the way she dries them off and treats their cuts and sores. As the puppies grow, licking remains a sign of acceptance, care giving or concern. There are similarities between this and being petted by a human, which seems to be interpreted as sign of acceptance, care giving and concern. Fast, frantic petting seems to excite dogs, while slow, dull petting seems to have a calming effect.

When the bitch begins to run out of milk and the puppies need solid food they begin licking the face of the bitch which stimulates her to regurgitate (vomit up) partially digested food which the pup takes right out of her mouth. Licking the face is therefore one of the first signals a puppy gives to an authority figure. As it grows, this is often used as a sign of respect for a higher ranking animal.

The bitch often reprimands the pup with an inhibited bite, which serves to warn the puppy without causing any actual damage. Older dogs often use the inhibited bite in a similar manner.

Visual

While all forms of communication are important, the greatest amount of information is transmitted visually. Dogs have a precise set of visual signals we have come to call body language. This is the segment of their communication system which is of greatest importance to the decoy. By using personal visual signals in the correct way, different forms of aggression can be triggered at exactly the time we need them for training purposes. Just as importantly, triggering any aggression at times must be avoided when it is inappropriate.

Reading the Dog

If you are already experienced at reading dogs you should probably stick with the method you use now. However, if you are new at the game, or do not have an established system for some reason, the following description will help get you started.

Try to look at all dogs in the same sequence so that all of them get uniform treatment. If you look at the head first one time and the tail first the next, you will eventually miss something important. Also remember to allow for physical causes. For instance, if there is a noise in front of the dog and he flicks his ears forward, it probably means he is listening and nothing more. At that point you will have to ignore the ears and read the rest of the body to find out how the dog feels about the thing listened to. If the dog is sick and slinks around slowly, it may mean it is feeling poorly physically, not that insecure about anything else. So always eliminate physical causes before you assign emotional meanings to a dog's body language.

It also helps to observe the large indicators first (such as the body stance) and then move to the smaller ones (like the ears and eyes). This can be done in a series of seven steps, beginning with energy level and moving on through body axis, stride muscle tone, neck, head and tail (see Text Box 3.1).

Text Box 3.1

**Seven Steps
of Reading a Dog**

1. Energy Level
2. Body Axis
3. Stride
4. Muscle Tone
5. Neck
6. Head
7. Tail

Energy Level

The energy level is often referred to as the state of arousal. The indicators of high energy are a wagging tail, barking, muscle tremors, faster reactions than usual and a tendency to walk faster or run when not under command. The low energy dog reacts slowly even when provoked and wants to stop and rest at every opportunity. This tells us nothing about the confidence level of the dog, but high energy dogs react more quickly and therefore can bite us faster and with less provocation. For your own safety it is wise to read the energy level first.

Steps two through seven should be read in the order listed, since they are listed in order of importance. In other words, information from each step is more important than information from any of the steps coming lower on the list. For example, if a dog is leaning away from a loud noise, but shows confidence in the head and tail, it is showing insecurity, no matter how good the head and tail look. Information from step two is more important than information from steps six and seven. A dog that shows insecurity in all three of the steps just mentioned is in much worse shape, but when signals give conflicting information, give more weight to the steps higher on the list. This will help you understand ambivalent dogs that send confusing sets of signals.

Those of you who already have an established pattern of reading the dog are probably not going to change your order of observation at this point in your career. My advice is to stay with the pattern you are comfortable with, but add the levels of importance from the seven steps when dogs give you ambivalent signals. If you teach beginner decoys, however, do them a favor and have them learn the seven steps in the order described above. In the long run, they will understand dogs better and read them faster.

Body Axis

The second thing we look at is the dog's body axis. Another way to think of this is where is the dog leaning? Bold, confident dogs stand straight upright or actually lean towards the object of attention. They often stay pointed straight at the object of attention. As they become more insecure or fearful, they begin to lean away from the source of their fear, actually walking backwards away from it in extreme cases (see figure 3.1).

They will also assume a more broadside alignment to the object of attention. This is the basis of "T ing up," where a submissive dog stands still in a sideways alignment to the approach of a dominant dog and allows the upper ranking animal to inspect it. The dominant dog faces and approaches the lower ranking dog perpendicularly from the side, usually at the shoulder, forming a letter T. This is a confident, dominant way to approach another animal. The submissive dog is required to remain stationary in the sideways alignment and let the upper ranking

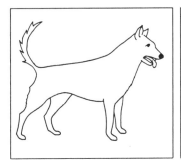  

Figure 3.1a   Figure 3.1b   Figure 3.1c

dog inspect it. If it does not do this, it is punished. If both dogs agree that one of them is dominant and the other submissive, no fight will ensue. However, if there is no agreement on who is dominant, the two dogs will jockey for position, each trying to "T up" on the other one, so that both keep moving in circles (see figure 3.2). This is often a sign that a fight of some sort is brewing.

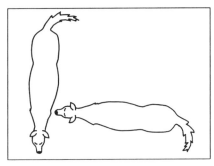 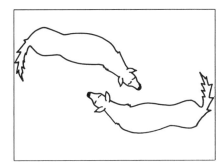

Figure 3.2a

Figure 3.2b

Stride

The third item of interest is the stride and leg movements. Dominant dogs approach submissive dogs. Submissive dogs only approach upper ranking dogs if they are giving numerous submissive signals to accompany such movement. The bold dog stands straight up or moves with long steps that hold the body up away from the ground. As the dog becomes more afraid, it begins to "slink" by shortening the stride and lowering the body closer to the ground, crawling at some point until in extreme cases it will actually lie down and roll over, lifting the upper hind leg to expose the genital area (see figure 3.3).

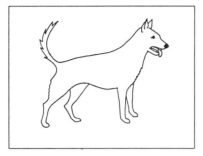

Figure 3.3a

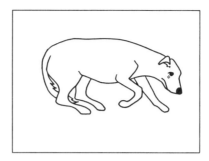

Figure 3.3b

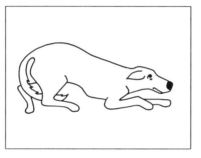

Figure 3.3c

Figure 3.3d

Some dogs will even urinate in this situation. A dominant dog will "stand over" a submissive dog to signal its power over it. This can be as little as putting its head or paw on top of the other dog's withers (top of the shoulders) as it Ts up or can actually mean that when the submissive dog lies down the dominant dog will literally stand with its body over the prostrate subordinate (see figure 3.4).

Figure 3.4a

Figure 3.4b

Beckoff's "play bow" is a lowering of the front end of the dog in a bouncing motion of the front legs to signal that whatever follows is not serious, but play (see figure 3.5). This is how dogs can tell if they are in a serious fight or a play fight. When it is play, someone bows first. Lifting of one of the front paws slightly off the ground appears to have different meanings depending upon the situation. After punishment by an upper ranking dog, it is a sign of submission. This is why if, during an obedience workout, your dog raises a paw after a correction, you do not want to get harder with it or you will create over-dominance problems. It is a very useful signal for trainers. On the other hand, some aggressive dogs lift a paw when they appear to be choosing between alternatives (often which way they will attack something). In this situation it may be a sign of momentary indecision (see figure 3.6).

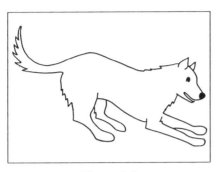

Figure 3.5

Figure 3.6a

Figure 3.6b

Muscle Tone

Muscle tone is the next important indicator. Walking with stiff leg movements is often practiced by dominant dogs threatening serious aggression while inspecting a lower ranking animal. On the other hand, fearful dogs will often exhibit muscle tremors, to the point where some appear to be shaking. At first glance this may seem to be contradictory, but it is not. Dogs who are truly confident in their ability to handle whatever situation they are getting into have loose, relaxed muscle tones. Tight muscle tone usually reflects something less than this complete level of confidence. For instance, if they are dominant, but not certain of their ability to maintain control, they will have to put on a good show, hence the stiff, strutting walk mentioned above. As their confidence levels drop, they exhibit more and more muscle tension until tremors become visible to the human eye. If you see no tremors, it is useful to put your hand on the chest of the dog between the front legs to test for them. This is particularly useful for handlers when testing the dog for gun shyness. Slight tremors, invisible to the human eye, can often be detected in this fashion and indicate slight insecurity. Occasionally a dog in high energy will have these tremors, but in this case there will be other indicators of high energy present.

Neck

The neck also gives us some information. Confident, dominant dogs approach an adversary with the neck and head high, often with an arch to the neck. Submissive dogs approach a leader with the neck and head in a low position. Frightened dogs carry their neck and head low also. The complication is that when dogs are stalking prey, the neck often carries the head low regardless of their confidence level, so the neck must be read in context with the overall situation.

Dogs are said to have their "hackles up" when the hair on the top of their necks sticks up, a condition scientists refer to as piloerection. Like curling the lip, this is an aggressive show designed to make them look bigger and scare another animal away. Similarly, it is considered a sign of stress, not of complete confidence.

Head

The next point of interest is the head. Direct eye contact is often a confident, dominant sign. Predators watch their prey carefully before they attack it and dominant dogs often try to stare down their opponents when trying to T up with them. Breaking eye contact is usually interpreted as a sign of submission during conflict. Sometimes they will actually turn the head away from the dominant animal as they stand sideways to its advance as the ultimate sign of breaking eye contact. An exception to this is when dogs in active conflict turn their heads to the side while still facing an adversary. At first it appears that they are submitting but in fact they are daring the opponent to come closer. Further inspection will show they are keeping an eye on the adversary and are not turning the body axis sideways in submission or giving any other submissive signals or, for that matter, any that would make an adversary go away. They are, in effect, luring the adversary into a trap. When the opponent comes close enough, they attack immediately. Many a new decoy has been bitten over the years by misreading this gesture (see figure 3.7).

Figure 3.7

The eyes also dilate when dogs get highly aggressive. At this point the tapetum, a reflective layer in the back of the eye, is more exposed than usual which gives the eyes an eery, crazed appearance. This is often referred to as "showing eye."

The ears also give us a look inside the dog's mind. The more confident dogs are, the more forward their ears will be carried. As they feel more insecure, the ears will be rotated back until they finally mold into the neck. Putting the ears back is also a sign of submission, so care must be used interpreting this sign. Many times dogs will submit to things that frighten them, in which case there is little difficulty interpreting the signals properly. However, it is also possible for dogs to feel confident and yet give you leadership rights, in which case the ears may be pulled back in submission while the rest of the body shows confidence.

Another complication is that when dogs make the decision to bite, they often prepare for the conflict by tucking their ears back into their neck, possibly to prevent damage to them in the upcoming fight. It is not a sign of fear or submission in this case, but merely a method of damage control. So while there are always exceptions, confident, dominant dogs generally hold their ears forward while fearful, submissive dogs pull their ears back (see figure 3.8).

Figure 3.8a, 3.8b, 3.8c, 3.8d

Curling the lips back to expose the teeth while growling has been vastly misinterpreted over the years. It is indeed a sign of aggression, but not always a sign of complete confidence. It is more an attempt to frighten the other dog and make it move away. Totally confident dogs have no need to make the other animal move away, they can handle anything that occurs right up close. Therefore, they stand their ground in confidence and allow you to approach, biting you if need be, but not trying to scare you away. So curling the lips to show the teeth is considered to be a sign of aggression based on insecurity (see figure 3.9).

Figure 3.9a

Figure 3.9b

Exposing only a few teeth in the front of the mouth is not considered a major problem, and dogs who do this are said to have a "short mouth" during aggression workouts. Others show more teeth, retracting the lips farther towards the back of the mouth. This is a sign of greater insecurity and such dogs are said to have a "long mouth" during aggression work. There is also a mimic grin which imitates the human smile. This is not common in breeds used for police work, but it does exist and functions as a greeting.

The mouth also gives an indication of relaxation or tension. When dogs are tense, they often hold their mouth tightly closed and breathe in a controlled manner, whereas relaxed dogs hold the mouth open and breath in a more spontaneous fashion. Licking the face of another animal is usually a sign of respect or care soliciting. When puppies are young and the milk supply of the bitch runs out, they begin to eat partially digested solid food which the bitch regurgitates. They stimulate her to bring this food back up by licking her face, so face licking is a manner of approaching a higher ranking animal when they need something from it.

Tail

The tail gives us a great deal of information. The most noticeable is the excitement level of the dog. When dogs become excited, they begin to wag their tails. Those with docked tails wag the stump and sometimes the entire rear end of their bodies. One of the reasons they may be excited is that they are greeting someone they like. Since that is what pet owners see the most, many people think that wagging the tail is a universal sign of friendship and greeting in dogs. This is not true. They will wag their tails any time they are excited. Many will wag their tails while they are biting you during a conflict. After all, that is exciting too.

The confidence level of dogs is often reflected in how they carry their tails (or the base of a docked tail). Generally, the higher the tails are carried, the more confident they are. As their confidence levels lower, so does the tail, until truly frightened dogs will actually tuck their tails between their legs. Some will even urinate at this point if they are over-stimulated. The tail is also used as an indicator of respect. Pictures of wolf packs show that only one animal carries its tail above the backbone. This is the dominant male (sometimes the dominant female will do this too). Everyone else in the pack carries their tail in a lower position. So carrying the tail high is a sign of confidence, dominance, or both (see figure 3.10).

Combining the above can give us some standard profiles of dogs in different emotional states. Figure 3.11 illustrates the appearance of a confident, dominant dog. It stands up straight and tall, faces the object of interest with direct eye contact, holds its ears forward, has loose muscle tone and a high tail carriage.

Figure 3.12 illustrates a confident dog which is signalling respect to an upper ranking animal. Note the same body postures as in Figure 3.11 except the ears are swept back. Sometimes the dog will look away

Figure 3.10

Figure 3.11

from the upper ranking animal to make sure it knows that no eye contact is being made.

Figure 3.13 shows an ambivalent dog, one which feels confidence and fear at the same time. Many combinations of postures are possible, the common denominator being that some of the signals will be showing confidence and others will show insecurity at the same time. Note in Figure 3.13 the dog shows confidence in all signals except the body axis, which is leaning backwards slightly and the tail, which is held roughly at the level of the backbone.

Figure 3.14 is an example of an insecure dog. The body is leaning back away from the object of interest, the stride is short, muscles are either tight or trembling, eye contact is broken, ears are swept back and the tail is low.

Figure 3.12

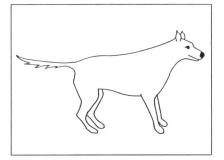

Figure 3.13

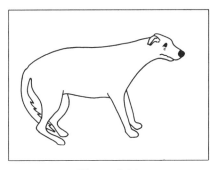

Figure 3.14

It would take too much time and space to chronicle the other possibilities here, but if you experiment with all possible combinations of the signals, you will be able to complete the list yourself. It is not a waste of time, reading dogs is a lifetime project. You never get good enough at it.

Most aspects of canine communication can be divided into three major categories which are important to decoys. One is distance increasing (go away), another distance decreasing (come here) and the third, arousal signals. The latter, or arousal signals merely show that the dog is excited (for example the tail wagging). To understand the other two divisions, keep in mind that dogs appear to have set up rules amongst themselves regarding their use. It seems that only upper ranking, or dominant dogs are allowed to use distance increasing signals when interacting with another dog. Lower ranking animals are not allowed to control the space around their bodies and are therefore not allowed to tell an upper ranking dog to get out of their space. If they do this by using distance increasing signals, they are punished by the dominant dog. Furthermore, they accept the punishment without complaint. It seems that lower ranking dogs are required to invite upper ranking dogs into their space and tolerate them there at any time. If the upper ranking dog traps them in its space, they are required to be extremely respectful and obedient while there. It is a sign of respect for the social position of the other dog. You do not have to agree with this approach yourself or think that it is fair; but if you want to understand dogs, you must accept that *they* agree on it. It maintains order and stability in their world. They set up the rules, not us. So try to remember that if you are giving distance increasing signals, you are speaking like an upper ranking dog, and if you are giving distance decreasing signals, you are speaking like a lower ranking animal. The same is true of a dog when it is speaking to you.

Distance Increasing Signals

Essentially all of the indicators of confidence described earlier are distance increasing signals and are designed to drive other dogs away or create fear and respect in them (see Text Box 3.2). A few, like the lip curl, raised hackles and stiff leg movements, betray a small amount of insecurity, but not much. They indicate a dog that is mostly confident, but not completely so.

To build a dog i.o challenge
aggressive dogs
do this.

ie: trained adults, test adults

Text Box 3.2

Distance Increasing Signals

1. **Facing the opponent**
2. **Movement or leaning towards the opponent**
3. **Standing up tall**
4. **Neck and head high**
5. **Hackles raised**
6. **Direct eye contact**
7. **Ears held forward**
8. **Lip curl and/or snarl**
9. **Tail held above back**
10. **Growl**
11. **Bark**

Distance Decreasing Signals

Conversely, all the signals of insecurity listed earlier are distance decreasing signals and are designed to show respect by inviting the upper ranking dog into the space of the dog exhibiting them (see Text Box 3.3).

These categories are of extreme importance to the decoy. By reading these signals carefully, a good decoy knows when to pressure a dog more and when limits are reached. Imitating distance increasing signals triggers a particular form of aggression in dogs, which we will discuss later. Imitating *you as a decoy do these to build confidence ↑ ie: pops, young n inexperienced dogs*

Text Box 3.3

Distance Decreasing Signals

1. Standing broadside
2. Movement or leaning away from opponent or standing still for inspection
3. Lowering body
4, Neck and head low
5. Hackles not raised
6. Breaking eye contact
7. Ears swept back
8. Absence of lip curl or snarl
9. Tail held below level of backbone
10. Whine
11. Absence of bark

distance decreasing signals in turn triggers a completely different form of aggression and combinations of the two trigger still different types. By sending different signals, the decoy can develop specific parts of a dog's aggressive make-up without over developing others.

4

Human-Canine Communication

Once you have learned to listen to what the dog is saying, it is time to learn how to speak back. Humans are somewhat limited in their ability to do this, since there are some canine signals which are difficult for us to imitate. For example, we cannot rotate our ears or put them forward and back as well as a dog can, no matter how hard we try. However, there are several canine signals we can imitate, which makes communication possible at a basic level.

Humans can bark, growl, whine and howl. The quality of these sounds is up for debate, but dogs will respond to our attempts to use these auditory forms of communication. This is why it is important for handlers not to use whiny tones of voice when giving commands or reprimands. Voice tones are extremely important since the dog probably doesn't understand the meaning of the words we use in most cases. What it understands is the noise itself (if repeated consistently) and whether it sounds like a growl (a threat) or a whine (a plea for help or acceptance usually made by a lower ranking animal to one of higher rank). Decoys cannot use the tones of voice, but can actually use the growls and whines themselves to great effect.

Olfactory communication is less valuable in most situations, since it is not socially acceptable for humans to mark their territory exactly the way dogs do. On occasion, humans have succeeded by putting white vinegar into small squirt bottles and marking their territory with that, but something is probably lost in translation.

Tactile communication encompasses many things, so be careful how you touch dogs. Petting and grooming are methods to express care and concern about a dog. As mentioned in chapter 3, humans can communicate excitement through the way they pet their dogs. Rapid movements signal high energy and excitement (and encourage the dog to assume the same condition), while slow, dull petting signals low energy and calmness (and encourages the dog to assume the same condition). Pinching the cheeks, ears or the skin in the flank area (what used to be called flanking) shows the intent to inflict pain and encourages suspicion and defensive reactions on the part of the dog. Humans don't bite dogs often, but when they do the dog clearly understands that they are unhappy about something (this is not recommended, since it is a good way to get your face bitten by an aggressive dog). They also understand you are unhappy when you shake them by the neck (when they are small enough), pinch the upper lip into the teeth or use two fingers to tap them on the nose. They quickly learn that striking causes pain and can easily identify the movements which lead up to it.

Dogs are the masters of body language, and we need to remember that they are always paying attention to what we are saying, even when we aren't. As handlers and trainers, we need to make our bodies say the same thing our voice is saying to reduce confusion on the dog's part. As decoys we need to be able to speak in nothing but body language in order to achieve the desired results with a minimum of stress placed on the dog.

The three major categories described in chapter 3 are particularly important for visual signals.

Arousal Signals

Arousal signals are expressed by the amount of energy we put into our movements. Wagging the tail is a bit difficult for us, so we have to be content with energy expression and barking type noises to signal a high state of arousal.

Distance Increasing Signals

Fortunately we can imitate distance increasing (go away) signals more effectively. The main problems we have are with raising our hackles (which we can't control voluntarily and don't show well when we can accomplish it), holding our ears in a forward position and holding our tail above the level of the back. The other signals listed in chapter 3 are possible which makes our list of major distance increasing signals a subset of those listed for dogs with the addition of fast movement of the appendages (hands, arms, feet and legs) once they learn that humans strike dogs (see Text Box 4.1).

Facing the dog imitates the dominant dog approaching the submissive dog. It also imitates a dog preparing to attack another animal. Dogs do not attack well sideways and usually square up on the target before rushing in to attack.

To challenge trained dogs to test a dog or aggressive

Text Box 4.1

Human Distance Increasing Signals

1. **Facing the opponent**
2. **Movement towards the opponent**
3. **Standing up tall**
4. **Neck and head high**
5. **Direct eye contact**
6. **Lip curl and/or snarl**
7. **Growl**
8. **Bark**
9. **Fast movements of the appendages**

When accompanied by other distance increasing signals, movement toward the opponent is also interpreted as a go away signal. Leaning towards the target is a low intensity signal, stepping towards it makes it more intense and actual walking or running towards it is the most intense form of the signal. Increasing the speed of this signal also increases its intensity, so we have an entire spectrum of intensities starting with the slow lean on the low intensity end, moving all the way up to the fast run on the most intense end. Again, this signal imitates the dominant dog who moves towards the submissive dog to inspect it. It also imitates the dog actually beginning an attack on another animal, since it has to move close enough to touch the opponent or prey before it can inflict any damage.

Standing up tall again imitates the dominant dog in its approach to the submissive dog. The dominant dog usually holds its body as high off the ground as possible with its neck and head held high also. This is where humans have an advantage. Standing on our hind legs, we can make ourselves look much taller than any dog. So standing up or crouching down can be used very effectively, with the higher postures being the more intense signals for increasing distance. Holding the neck and head high constitutes a distance increasing signal for similar reasons and for the additional reason that lowering the head and neck often breaks eye contact.

Direct eye contact serves to increase distance for the same reasons as the above described signals. It is nearly always a component of the dominant dog's approach or an actual attack. Attack, in particular, is usually preceded by close visual inspection of the target, searching for possible weaknesses. A good point to remember with this signal is that humans often wear sunglasses, which prevents the dog from seeing exactly what we are looking at. Many decoys have developed the habit of turning their entire head when they break eye contact, so that it is readily apparent when they reestablish it by turning the head back.

Lip curling and snarling are almost as difficult to get humans to do as growling and barking. It just isn't socially acceptable for us to go around making dog faces and noises. It certainly is not the sort of thing most parents encourage in their children and it seems to be a lesson we have remembered. None the less, they are very effective signals when interacting with dogs. It's probably wise not to use them when your parents or in laws are in town, though.

An important point to remember is that you do not have to actually strike dogs to teach them that fast appendage movements are distance increasing signals. If fast hand and foot movements are paired with the other go away signals, they will soon be accepted as part of the collection of distance increasing signals. Soon thereafter the mere raising of a hand will be recognized as a precursor to go away signals and will become one itself. No one should use this item as an excuse to abuse dogs in the name of aggression training.

Text Box 4.2

Human Distance Decreasing Signals

1. **Turning body sideways**
2. **Movement away from opponent or standing still for inspection**
3. **Lowering body**
4. **Neck and head held low**
5. **Breaking eye contact**
6. **Absence of lip curl or snarl**
7. **Whine**
8. **Absence of bark**
9. **Slow or no movements of appendages**

Distance Decreasing Signals

The distance decreasing (come here) signals obviously have the reverse function of the increasing signals. It should be no surprise, then, that in most cases they are simply the opposite of the distance increasing signals (see Text Box 4.2).

Turning the body sideways imitates the stance of the submissive dog being inspected by the upper ranking dog. It is also a stance from which one cannot attack an object at a distance efficiently, so it is less of a threat than facing the dog squarely.

Movement out of the space of an upper ranking animal shows respect for its position in the pack. So to move back away from a dominant dog is a gesture of submission, and invites the upper ranking dog to come over to you. There is also a desire on the part of a pack animal to maintain contact with the pack. When others move away from it, a dog is tempted to go in that direction to ensure that it does not get left behind. In addition to this, there is a predatory response in dogs that tempt many of them to follow and pursue things that try to move away from them. If movement away from the upper ranking dog is not possible or desirable, the alternative for the submissive dog is to stand still for inspection and give submissive gestures with the rest of the body.

Lowering the body imitates the submissive or frightened dog that bends its legs to the point of putting its belly on the ground before rolling over. This is why it is such a confidence builder to let a dog knock the decoy down when you start a new phase of its work or when it has had a bad experience. The effect of seeing the opponent fall down and stay down in submission so that the dog ends up being taller or able to actually stand over the defeated enemy is great. To appear weak to the dog, decoys have been known to work them on their knees, to appear shorter. When the dog is muzzled properly, they have been known to work dogs flat on their backs to let them keep knocking them back down and stand over them until their confidence reaches acceptable levels (at which point they move on to other things).

Holding the neck and head low imitates the submissive dog being inspected and is the opposite of the head carriage of the upper ranking dog. It also gives the appearance of breaking eye contact. Breaking eye contact is another submissive signal used by any dog showing respect for an upper ranking dog.

Figure 4.1

The whine is a plea for assistance, usually made by a lower ranking dog to a dominant one. It clearly shows you to be submissive.

Using the above gestures it is possible for a human to be established as either a dominant or submissive animal, or one that fluctuates between the two. For instance, figure 4.1 shows a human giving all distance increasing signals, and is therefore advertising as a dominant animal. Note he is facing us directly; moving our direction; standing up as tall as possible with neck and head held high; looking directly at us; snarling with lips curled; and what the picture can't show us is that the growling (at the times when not snarling) and moving arms in quick, jerky motions. The decoy is telling us quite clearly that he is dominant and that we had better get out of his space, stand submissively for inspection, roll over submissively, or fight. Also note that with the exception of the lip curl, growl and fast arm movements, this is precisely how the average person approaches a strange dog. Small wonder that most of them get bitten when the dog is dominant or easily frightened.

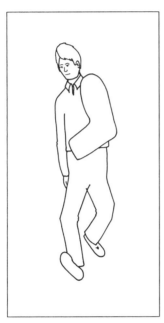

Figure 4.2

Figure 4.2 shows a human giving fewer distance increasing signals. In fact, ambivalent signals are being given, in that some are distance increasing and some are distance decreasing. Note that the shoulders are rotated slightly, eye contact has been broken and there is no lip curl. This is much less of a challenge to dominant dogs and less frightening to the weak of heart. The intensity of the threat can be lowered further by making whining noises rather than being silent or making deep growling noises. Advertising as a less dominant animal, but not necessarily submissive, who does not intend to attack at the moment is the message.

Figure 4.3 shows a human giving all distance decreasing signals. Note that the body is rotated slightly sideways; standing still for inspection (he could also be moving away from us or lying down); knees are slightly bent which lowers the body; neck and head are held lower than normal; and eye contact has been broken. What the picture can't show is that the arms and legs are still and the decoy is either silent or making whining type noises. The only way stronger signals could be given would be to lower the body farther or move away from us. The

Figure 4.3

message is of a submissive animal and is inviting us into this space. We are free to approach as we wish. This human is no threat to us either physically or socially.

Decoy prospects should practice these signals intensively, until they can switch from increasing to decreasing signals in a split second with no errors. They should be able to give all increasing signals except for one decreasing signal (and vice versa) and then change the contrary signal for another, one at a time without changing the overall effect of what they are saying to the dog. They should be able to give half increasing and half decreasing signals in several combinations without stopping to think about it. This is the language of the decoy. It is what sets the decoy apart from people who merely take bites. Only when you are master of it can you possibly reach your potential as a decoy. If possible, you should master it before you begin training. If you are already an experienced decoy, mastering it will only improve your skill and worth. Any way you look at it, it is time well spent.

5

Canine Aggression

Decoys need to do more than just stimulate aggression in the dogs they are helping to train. They must stimulate the correct form of aggression at the correct time in the correct amounts. In order to do this they must be familiar with the different types of aggression which occur in dogs and what body language will trigger each of them. In this chapter we will discuss the origins of aggression, the different forms of aggression and whether or not they are useful in the training of police service dogs.

Studies in other species have indicated that aggression is regulated by activity in certain areas of the brain, mostly the hypothalamus and the amygdala. By stimulating certain areas scientists have been able to create two types of aggression. One seems to be connected with the gathering of food and the other with excitement of emotional responses. The food gathering behavior (predatory aggression) can be produced by electrical stimulation of that area of the brain called the lateral hypothalamus and can be inhibited by activity in the ventromedial hypothalamus. It involves low key, quiet body language and stalking approaches which minimize distance increasing signals (see chapters 3 and 4 for discussions of these). Its main purpose is the capture and death of the target animal and is characterized by bites to the neck, throat and head area.

Other types of aggression seem to involve the autonomic system, which affects things like heart rate, blood pressure, pupil dilation, raised hackles, etc., and have been called "affective" forms of aggression. Some can be produced by electrical stimulation of the medial hypothalamus in the brain and are characterized by numerous distance influencing signals and in some cases a lot of noise. The damage inflicted by affective aggression is often serious, even fatal, but is not intended primarily to kill as the ultimate goal. Electrical stimulation of the amygdala section of the brain reduces the amount of stimulation needed in the hypothalamus to produce aggression, so it may be involved with both these forms of aggression.

As with many behaviors, aggression begins in the genetic make-up of the dog. The physical structures of the brain mentioned in the preceding paragraph are developed and controlled by genetic factors. Chemicals and hormones also effect its expression. Injections of acetylcholine into the hypothalamus can produce affective forms of aggression in some species, while increased levels of serotonin in the brain seem to reduce aggressive responses. The influence of chemicals on the nervous system, particularly in regards to aggression, is not well defined at this time. Much work is being done on the chemical basis of behavior, though, and the next ten years should show radical increases in our knowledge of the subject. It is a topic that dog trainers should keep their eye on.

The effect of male hormones (androgens) on aggression is well known. They seem to have nothing to do with predatory aggression, but scientists feel that the presence of androgens in the brain during puppy development increases the potential for affective aggression when the animal matures. Because of this, more males show high levels of aggression as adults than females (except when females are protecting their puppies). Unfortunately, this has lead to the belief that only intact males (with testicles) have enough aggression for police work. This is not true. Once the aggressive responses have been learned and properly maintained, a male dog can be castrated and still perform as well as before. Certain females and castrated males have strong aggressive tendencies and make good police dogs. Trends are nice when dealing with large numbers of dogs, but when working with individuals, remember there are always notable exceptions. If you would not judge a book by its cover, do not judge a dog by its breed, sex, size or color. Before we launch into descriptions of the various forms of aggression, it might be useful to divide them into two categories, "affective" and "non-affective" (see Text Box 5.1).

Text Box 5.1

Types of Canine Agression

Affective

1. Territorial
2. Pain induced
3. Fear induced
4. Intermale
5. Social (Dominance)
6. Protective
7. Maternal
8. Learned
9. Redirected
10. Irritable

Non-Affective

11. Sexual
12. Predatory
13. Play
14. Idiopathic

Territorial

Territorial is the first form of affective aggression. It is extremely prevalent in dogs, and is so important that it can reverse dominance relationships. Many dogs are much more dominant and confident on their own territory than they are somewhere else. This is why good trainers always test candidates on strange territory (police dogs rarely work at home, they are usually working on someone else's turf). The space around a dog is divided into several categories: home range;

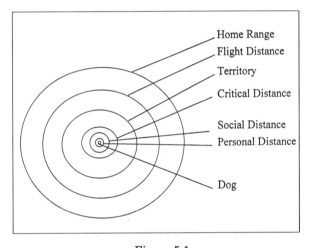

Figure 5.1

territory; social space; and personal space (see figure 5.1). There is also a flight distance and a critical distance. The territory is considered to be the area which the dog is willing to defend. Some dogs have such a high genetic predisposition to this type of aggression that they will become aggressive the moment you cross their territorial line, regardless of what your body language is. This makes it a very useful form of aggression for police training in the initial stages of protection work. All we have to do is set the dog up the same spot enough times for it to consider that place its territory and then physically jump back and forth across the border to stimulate aggression. However, if it cannot be managed properly, it can become a disadvantage at the more advanced stages of training. Some dogs need encouragement to respond this way (in the form of body language) and some are not interested in defending territory at all unless strongly provoked. The boundaries of a dog's territory can be well defined in the form of a fence, the borders of the car they are in, or a road. However, the line is often unseen visually, which leads some people to think that it is imaginary. To fully appreciate dogs you must accept that the line is very real to them and they always seem to know exactly where it is, even though we have trouble keeping track of it.

Pain Induced

Pain induced aggression is common in practically all domestic species of animal, and the dog is no exception. Dogs have individual tolerances to pain, so the speed and severity of their reaction to it can vary from animal to animal. Pain is the basis of the old form of stimulation known as flanking, where the decoy would approach the dog calmly, or even in a friendly manner, grasp the skin of the dog in the flank area just in front of the hind legs, pinch and twist the skin as hard as possible while getting back before the dog could bite him. The dog would instinctively bite at the source of the pain and see that aggression could make the source of the pain go away. Some people still use this method, while some pinch the ears or the cheeks and others use sticks or whips to get the same results. It is a fast method of bringing out aggression and works well in some dogs. However, it does not work well in a large number of dogs and is no longer recommended as a standard technique for dogs beginning training. Small children, for instance, often do horrible things to dogs just out of curiosity (and usually when their parents can't see what they are doing). Infants and small children should never be left alone with working dogs. It is too easy for the children to inflict pain on the dog without realizing what they are actually doing. And dogs that have been flanked will react quickly and decisively to such treatment.

Pain is also part of the basis for what trainers refer to as the "defensive drive" of dogs. It teaches several things. One, that the proper response to pain is aggression. This is not always the case, as when a child grabs the dogs coat or ears during a public relations demonstration. Or when your young daughter trips and falls on the dog while it is asleep. Or when the veterinarian has to handle it or give an injection. The list can go on, but the point is clear – aggression is not always the proper response to pain. Pain also teaches the dog that working with humans is not fun but very serious business. Triggering too much pain induced aggression too early in a dog's training often produces a dog that has difficulty relaxing and being confident in its abilities to handle any situation.

Confident dogs who have had too much pain induced aggression triggered will give ambivalent signals and are easy to recognize. They look much like other confident, aggressive dogs except they show a lot of lip curl and snarling along with raised hackles and the stiff, tense leg movements described in chapter 3 as signs of minor insecurity. Insecure dogs who have too much pain induced aggression triggered appear just like other insecure, aggressive dogs and are indeed fear biters. So the ability to handle pain induced aggression must be developed carefully. Too much emphasis on it creates dogs of limited value. While they can complete basic assignments, they often become too stressed out to be good at the advanced levels of police training. Consequently, many trainers prefer to begin working with other forms of aggression first, leaving work on pain induced for later in training. Then after the dog has learned confidence through less stressful methods, they start triggering pain induced aggression, but just enough to create balance between it and the other forms.

The third thing that flanking and other painful techniques teach is that humans cannot be trusted. They will often approach in a friendly manner as a ruse to set you up for an attack. Consequently, dogs should not let humans approach them. This is a two edged sword. Some handlers prefer a dog that no one can approach (most of them work in bad areas of the inner cities where admittedly the environment is more hostile than it is for many officers). They seem to be in the minority now though, as most officers see unapproachable dogs as an unnecessary liability. The trend now seems to be towards dogs that are approachable and safe when the officer has to interact with the public. The ability to handle pain induced aggression should be accomplished carefully and always in balance with the other forms of aggression. If it becomes the primary focus of training, you will limit the dog when it comes to the advanced levels of training, and in many cases expose yourself to unnecessary liabilities.

Fear Induced

Fear induced aggression is a response to something which frightens the dog. Many dogs do not have the genetic make-up to withstand threats or pressure. They will do their best to submit to the frightening object or animal, but if these attempts do not remove the fear of the situation they resort to other measures. When the threat reaches the flight distance (see figure 5.1) they escape if that is physically possible. If that is not an option and the threat keeps approaching, they will take action when the threat reaches the critical distance (see figure 5.1) The more passive and submissive ones will lie down, roll over and hope for mercy. Others seem to make the decision that it is time to fight, even though they don't want to. This is the classic fear biter, bane of all veterinarians and kennel workers. If given the chance, they would much rather escape than fight. But if they see no way out, they will fight with ferocity, doing whatever damage is necessary to make the fear go away. That is the key – remember that fear is the root of this type of aggression. Remove the fear and the aggression will disappear. It has some similarities to pain induced aggression because sometimes it is the fear of pain that the dog is reacting to. However, sometimes the dog is frightened of something that has never inflicted pain on it, so we cannot call this pain induced aggression.

Neophobia (the fear of new, or strange things) can trigger this type of aggression as well as startling confrontations in which no contact is made but in which the dog is taken by surprise. Decoys who use signals or approaches that are too strong for a dog can drive it into this type of aggression by mistake. This is usually an error and the sign of a low quality decoy if it happens frequently. Fear induced aggression is another part of what trainers call the "defensive drive" of a dog, so it should be used as carefully as anything else connected to the defensive drive (review the cautions listed under pain induced aggression – most of them apply to fear induced as well). Many people think that dogs with high levels of fear induced aggression make good police dogs. This is not usually true. The classic fear biter will often break and run when given the chance and is not a reliable protector. It is mostly interested in feeling less afraid, and escape will accomplish that.

Intermale

Intermale aggression is that which is restricted to male to male conflict. It is not general competition for rank in the pack, which can involve females, but aggression shown by a male dog and specifically aimed at any other male dog. It is never directed at females. It is the source of much of the dog fighting problems trainers encounter and as such is not terribly useful to police dog trainers. It is something which should be tested for before a dog enters training.

Social

Social aggression (sometimes referred to as dominance aggression) serves to maintain order in the pack. It is the mechanism by which disagreements regarding social rank are ultimately settled. There are two basic types of dominant dogs. One is what I call actively dominant, which is a dog that immediately seeks a leadership position when placed into a strange group of dogs (and will fight to attain it), responds actively to any challenge by a lower ranking dog and will let no sign of disrespect go unanswered. The other is what I call passively dominant, in that it does not consider any other animal to be higher ranking, but sees no reason to fight over it. They tend to ignore most signs of disrespect from others but will not show respect for anyone else, either. In some instances, it is easy to mistake them for low ranking dogs, until it is too late. The actively dominant dog often shows a high level of social aggression. This is the basis of what many trainers call "fight drive" since these dogs will fight any time they don't get exactly what they want. After all, the rules of the dog world seem to be that dominant animals get everything they want. Any lower ranking dog that doesn't give them exactly what they want deserves to be punished. This is an extremely useful form of aggression for police trainers. All they have to do is to convince the dog that the handler and maybe one other person are the top ranking animals, that the dog comes next, and that everyone else in the world is below them in rank. The dog will then obey the handler (and one other person in case the handler is ever down or incapacitated) but instantly fight anyone else in the world at the handler's bidding. Confident body language will be shown.

Protective

Protective aggression can be confused with social aggression. Sometimes dominant dogs fight to maintain possession of something, but that is really a way of defending their rank. Protective aggression can occur in lower ranking dogs, who are not trying to take a leadership position. They select something and protect it while making no efforts to increase their social position. Sometimes they protect another dog, sometimes a human and sometimes an object. This form of aggression is useful in some dogs whose other forms of aggression are poorly developed but have a favorite person. Sometimes they will show aggression to protect the handler but not to defend themselves or gather food.

As such it is a useful form of aggression but many trainers feel that it should be strongly supported by other types.

Maternal

Maternal aggression involves the female protecting her puppies. It is often felt that the male is more aggressive than the female, but this is not the case when considering maternal aggression. Normally friendly bitches can be transformed once they have puppies. They become some of the most aggressive animals you will ever meet. It pays to be careful around first time mothers until you get some idea of how they are coping with the new experience. One of the more interesting versions of this type of aggression occurs when the bitch is pseudopregnant. This is a bitch that is not pregnant, but has a hormonal imbalance that makes her think she is. She will often pick an object, such as a shoe or sock, and treat it just like a real puppy. She will even produce milk for it in some cases. If you walk in to get your shoe or sock back, she may react with severe maternal aggression. While this is interesting, maternal aggression has no real value in training police dogs.

Learned

Learned aggression can begin as any of the other forms. Once the aggression has been sufficiently rewarded and maintained, it becomes a learned response and no longer requires the original stimuli to trigger it, merely a cue from the handler or the decoy. Sometimes this happens with no cue from the humans and a reward that occurs by accident. This causes problems for pet owners, but learned aggression is quite prevalent in police training. In fact, most of what we teach becomes learned at some point. In the early stages of training, though, it is not something that a decoy can trigger naturally.

Redirected

Redirected aggression occurs when another form of aggression cannot be expressed. For instance, when the dog really wants to bite a dominant dog (or human) but does not dare to do so. It frequently redirects the aggression to a lower ranking dog and bites it instead of the dominant dog (who originally triggered the aggression). Frequently the recipient will turn and take it out on the next dog down the line, and so on. This type of aggression can be observed when handlers irritate dogs during protection work. The dog doesn't really want to bite his master, but is being stimulated, so it redirects the aggression to the nearest animal of lower rank, the decoy. So instead of sitting and barking as wished by the handler, it runs in and takes a dirty bite to avoid getting into real trouble by biting the handler.

Irritable

Irritable aggression occurs when something irritates the dog enough to make it aggressive. Mostly these dogs just want to be left alone. The source of the irritation usually goes away, which rewards the dog for such behavior. It is more likely to occur when dogs are sick or hungry and less tolerant of disturbances. As we saw in the last paragraph, excited dogs who are intent on doing something and have an incompetent handler can become irritated enough to bite. Older dogs are more prone to irritable aggression than they were as younger dogs. This can be a problem in retired service dogs who are less tolerant of nuisances and have had extensive bite training. Generally this is not a useful type of aggression for police work, but decoys can fuss with dogs like this by rubbing the hair on their face against the grain and doing other annoying things until they snap at them. With enough reward it can become learned aggression, but often it is not worth the time invested.

Sexual

Sexual Aggression is the first form of non-affective aggression. It is related directly to mating. Often the female is not receptive and wants the male to leave her alone. If he doesn't, she will become aggressive to make her point. Sometimes the male will become aggressive to maintain control of a receptive female. In essence, any aggression which is connected to the act of mating would be considered sexual aggression. It is generally not a useful form of aggression for police dog training.

Predatory

Many scientists consider this form of aggression merely a form of food gathering behavior. None the less, it is extremely useful in training police dogs. This is a low stress type of aggression, where the dog chases a small, non threatening animal that runs away from it. If the dog chooses the correct sort of prey, there is not much of a fight at the end of the chase and nothing to be frightened of. This is the basis of what trainers call the "prey drive" in dogs. It gives them the desire to chase decoys and apprehend them, once the dog is confident in its ability to beat decoys. As such it is a crucial aspect of police dog training. However, it should not be over emphasized. For instance, it is possible to train sport dogs to score highly in competition manwork using only predatory aggression. The dogs become what we call sleeve happy and have no intention of getting into a real fight.

If predatory aggression has been over emphasized in a dog's training, it will not do well on the street. The trick to this is to balance predatory aggression with pain induced, fear induced and social aggression so that the dog is strong in all three (prey, defense and fight drives). Some sport trainers do this and some do not. This is why some sport dogs can be easily converted to police dogs and some cannot. It all depends on their genetic make-up and how their first trainers developed aggression in them. Predatory aggression is also one of the problems that many pet dogs have with children. Children have quick, jerky movements, love to squeal like prey species and run away, and are about the right size to be considered a prey object. Infants and small children should never be left alone with working dogs. They are masters at triggering aggression in dogs. I often tell decoy candidates to study the movements and actions of children. Children are the best natural decoys in the world, unfortunately.

Play

Play aggression is a way for young dogs to practice adult fighting skills which will be important later in life without having to hurt each other. In young adults it is still present but nearly always preceded by Beckoff's play bow from one of the participants. Once that signal is given, so everyone involved understands that what follows is play, some of the most ferocious looking things can happen, but all bites will be inhibited so that no damage results to any participants. This can scare the daylights out of owners, but is apparently quite entertaining for the dogs. This type of aggression can be useful in police training when we make mistakes. For instance, when a decoy triggers too much defensive aggression in a young dog there can be confidence problems. One way a decoy can alleviate the problem caused is to play bow to the dog, suggesting that the dog misunderstood him and that what just happened was actually play. After a certain amount of play type aggression, the dog's confidence will return and it can be returned to the more serious defensive aggression, but this is usually done at a later time.

Idiopathic

The last form of aggression to be discussed is difficult to categorize and is listed here because I'm not quite sure where else it belongs. Idiopathic aggression is that which has no known or definable origin. The origin exists, we just don't know what it is. Many times it is caused by some tumor in the nervous system or brain itself. Sometimes it is a chemical imbalance in the brain. Often the cause cannot be determined until the dog is dead and a necropsy can be performed. Dogs affected by this type of aggression are usually unpredictable and extremely dangerous to work with. Their aggression cannot be controlled reliably and you never know what might trigger an aggressive reaction. Sometimes there is no triggering stimulus that we can identify. This type of aggression is of no use to police dog trainers. Dogs showing this type of aggression should be eliminated from police training.

So the aggressive make-up of a dog is composed of many separate factors. Trainers need to balance these factors in particular mixtures to get the best possible results. For them to do this, they need decoys who can trigger individual types of aggression on demand without triggering others. When aggression control work begins, they need decoys who can quickly stop triggering any aggression at all. This requires knowledge of the above plus what sort of body language will trigger each form of aggression; and then the discipline to practice enough to master the subject. It takes many years to become a good decoy, as opposed to being someone who just takes bites to help out.

6

Stimulating Canine Aggression

In chapter 4 we learned how to present ourselves as dominant, frightening animals, or submissive, non-threatening ones. This was accomplished by using distance increasing and decreasing signals in different combinations. In chapter 5 we learned there are fourteen different types of aggression in dogs. Now it is time to combine this information by pairing the useful types of aggression with the sort of signals that stimulate them. In general, we want to remember that in the world of dogs, only upper ranking animals are allowed to use distance increasing signals since they are the only ones allowed to control the space around them. Consequently distance increasing signals are considered to be challenging, fear provoking or mentally pressuring (see Text Box 3.2 in chapter 3 and Text Box 4.1 in chapter 4).

In contrast, lower ranking or frightened dogs use distance decreasing signals so the upper ranking dog knows they are not challenging them or trying to control the space around them. Consequently distance decreasing signals are considered to be submitting, non threatening, or pressure releasing (see Text Box 3.3 in chapter 3 and Text Box 4.2 in chapter 4). To engage in a confrontation and force the opponent to release pressure with those sort of signals seems to be extremely rewarding to dogs, so distance decreasing signals are often used at times when we wish to reward a dog for a particularly good performance.

Territorial

Territorial aggression is stimulated by the decoy moving into and out of the dog's territory or space. Dogs with strong territorial aggression don't care what type of body language the decoy is using, it is the crossing of the border that stimulates them. Strangely enough they often don't mind you being in their territory or space half as much as they mind you crossing the border in order to approach them. It is sometimes better to stay farther away from them, so you can jump back and forth over the line more frequently (see figure 6.1). If the dog retains confident body language, the decoy can use distance increasing signals as he crosses the border, but when the dog has reacted properly, the decoy should jump back across the border giving distance decreasing signals. As noted before, this rewards the dog and increases its confidence. The ultimate reward though, for territorial aggression, is to see

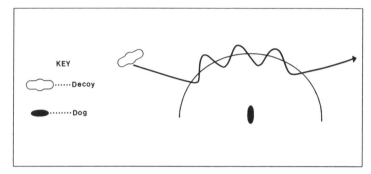

Figure 6.1

the enemy leave the territory. Therefore, at the end of the session, the decoy should run away, leaving the dog master of his territory.

Pain Induced

Pain induced aggression can be stimulated with any method that inflicts pain and allows the decoy to get away safely. Methods of flanking were noted in the previous chapter where it was also noted that many trainers only stimulate this form of aggression after the dog has had other less stressful forms developed. When the dog is confident and working well, small amounts of pain are introduced with something like a light stick. The dog is always rewarded by the decoy running away after it shows aggression to the pain. Remember that the removal of pain is the reward for this type of aggression, not merely getting a bite. If a bite makes the pain go away, it is the bite that is rewarded, and it is the going away of pain that is the actual reinforcement.

Fear Induced

Fear Induced aggression can be stimulated by the decoy using body language that is too strong (has too many or too severe distance increasing signals in it for what the dog can handle at the moment) (see figure 6.2). If only a small amount of fear is produced, and the decoy quickly changes to distance decreasing signals and runs away, the dog

Figure 6.2

will profit from it by learning that it need not fear humans who give such signals. Fear induced aggression can also be stimulated by anything else that frightens the dog, such as decoys ambushing the dog by jumping out in a threatening manner while it is unprepared (for instance when it is being taken for a walk between training sessions). This is why trainers have used such techniques for so long to test a dog's ability to handle fearful situations. Some trainers test canine candidates in this manner immediately and only train the survivors, while others save the technique for later in training when the dog's confidence levels are at maximum.

Both methods work. Anything that makes the dog suspicious will stimulate a mild form of fear induced aggression, since suspicion is effectively a mild form of fear. This is why some decoys dress and move strangely until the dog alerts in their direction and then run away (see figure 6.3). It is very effective in suggesting the presence of something frightening and then teaching the dog that it need not fear the strange thing after all, since one good bark will make it run away. If only small amounts of fear are generated by the above described techniques and each experience concludes with the dog victorious, the dog's confidence increases. If too much fear is generated by any of these methods, the dog will become more insecure and too many experiences of this type will produce a dog with an over developed "defensive drive." As noted before, these dogs are of limited use in police work since they are too stressed out for advanced maneuvers. Introducing the dog to potentially frightening situations is important in the training of a police service dog, but it must be done carefully to avoid creating fear biters. The reward for this type of aggression is the lowering of fear levels in the dog. This can usually be accomplished by letting the dog see the frightening stimulus (the decoy) run away. Again, a bite is not necessarily the reward. The removal of fear is the reinforcement.

Figure 6.3a   Figure 6.3b

Social

Social aggression can be stimulated by establishing the decoy as a lower ranking animal and then challenging the dog's rank in the pack by giving some distance increasing signals to it. As we mentioned earlier, this violates the rules of the dog world, and it is the responsibility of the upper ranking dog to punish the rude lower ranking dog (in this case, the decoy). This is one of the ways they maintain order and stability in the pack. If the dog has a strong predisposition to social aggression, the decoy need only challenge it by using distance increasing signals and the dog will react swiftly and strongly. If the dog has a lesser predisposition for this type of aggression, the decoy must first give as many distance decreasing signals as possible when he interacts with the dog, which establishes him in time as a lower ranking animal.

Once this has been established, the decoy begins to give a few distance increasing signals. For instance, he might actually turn and look into the dog's eyes for a second, then break eye contact and resume distance decreasing signals (see figures 6.4, 6.5 and 6.6). If the dog does not respond, the number and intensity of distance increasing signals are increased (always followed by distance decreasing signals to show underlying insecurity) until the dog reacts aggressively. At the first sign of aggression from the dog, the decoy runs away giving as many distance decreasing signals as possible. Several repetitions of this will convince the dog that the decoy is a rude coward who can be easily beaten. After a while the dog will be willing to fight harder and harder to win, knowing that if he just fights long and hard enough, he can always beat the decoy.

Figure 6.4

Figure 6.5

Figure 6.6

The reward for this type of aggression is the establishment of the dog as the upper ranking animal. However, the signals that show submission are also the ones that stimulate predatory aggression (see below). Consequently, by switching to the distance decreasing signals used in predatory aggression, the decoy can reward the dog for fighting well in social aggression. If a bite is what leads to the other animal signalling submission, then the bite is rewarded, but keep in mind that it is the signalling of submission by the adversary that is the actual reward.

Predatory

Predatory aggression can be stimulated by imitating the movements of prey animals. Most prey species run away when attacked and often give distance decreasing signals when caught. So objects that move quickly away from or across the front of dogs tend to stimulate

Figure 6.7

this form of aggression. Often decoys tie tug toys to the ends of ropes or leashes and drag them on the ground behind them angling slightly away from the dog to encourage it to chase after the toy and catch it. If the dog is successful, it is allowed to carry the prize around and show off a little (see figure 6.7).

The decoys use distance decreasing signals during this drill and encourage the dog to play tug of war before they release the toy. Eventually a burlap sack is used and then placed on a protective sleeve, which the decoy allows to slip off as soon as the dog bites it. The dog then gets to carry the sleeve around to show off. Since fast movement away from the dog is actually one of the "come here" signals, we can see that maximum use of distance decreasing signals is what stimulates predatory aggression. The reward for this type of aggression is the simulation of death by the prey object or decoy. This is why the dog enjoys prancing around with the "dead" sleeve or tug toy in its mouth so much. If this is not possible, the decoy should feign death from time to time to reward the dog.

Combining Types of Aggression

Decoys can use combinations of these approaches to suit the individual temperament of each dog they work. If one dog has too much fear induced aggression in evidence, the decoy can switch to distance decreasing signals and work the dog using predatory aggression. After predatory aggression has been increased to the point that it balances the fear induced aggression, the dog can be worked normally, since its stress levels will now be under control. Conversely, if a dog works all in predatory aggression, and can't handle fear induced aggression well, the decoy can switch to distance increasing signals and gradually build the fear induced aggression of the dog to where it balances the predatory component. Again, once this balance has been reached, the dog can be worked normally.

Often it will be best to use both increasing and decreasing signals in the same session, as when you are working with fight drive. You simply use more of the type the dog needs to develop properly. Sometimes you want to use all three types of aggression in the same workout. If you prefer to work with social aggression, but the dog also has a problem handling fear induced aggression, you could use a mixture of signals, emphasizing the distance increasing signals to develop the fear induced aggression more fully. If you wished to develop predatory aggression more fully, you could use social aggression, emphasizing the distance decreasing signals to develop predatory aggression more fully. Some trainers like to work one type of aggression for a period of time, then bring it to a peak and switch to another type and work that for a while. This switching of types in the same workout is sometimes called "channelling the dog."

Understanding which signals trigger which type of aggression gives the decoy the ability to adjust second by second to what the dog needs. He simply reads the dog's body language and reacts with the proper signals. This is far superior to decoying in set patterns simply because that's the way you were originally taught to do it and don't know any other formula. Decoying should never be a formula. It should be a dynamic process of communication that adjusts to each dog's needs as they develop.

New decoys are frequently confused regarding the type of aggression they have stimulated when working a dog. For instance, the trainer has told them to work the dog in "fight drive" (which really means to stimulate more social aggression than anything else) but they are not sure if that is what they are actually doing. The keys to this are: 1) what signals the decoy is using and 2) the body language of the dog. If the decoy is predominantly using distance decreasing signals and the body language of the dog indicates confidence, you are most likely seeing predatory aggression. Many trainers would say that at this point you are working the dog in "predatory drive" or simply "prey drive." If the decoy is using distance increasing signals and the body language of the dog is completely confident, you are probably seeing social aggression. Many trainers would call this working the dog in "fight drive." If at any time you see insecurity or fear in the dog's body language, you are probably looking at fear induced or pain induced aggression, or some combination of both. You would then be working the dog in what many trainers call "defensive drive," or just plain "defense drive."

So your ability to know which form of aggression you have stimulated is dependent upon your ability to read the dog's body language. Additionally, your ability to stimulate the particular type of aggression the trainer wants is dependent upon your ability to use your own body to give the correct signals at the correct strength at the correct time.

7

Basic Skills

Decoys inevitably develop their own styles of working, which leads to great variation in the specific techniques which are actually employed in the field. However, if you observe enough good decoys, you will begin to see certain common denominators. While it is beyond the scope of this book to list all the different techniques used, it would be quite useful to discuss some of the skills and items that are basic to most of them.

Proper Mind Set

Safety consciousness is the first important skill. There are many risks involved with decoying. Some of these are avoidable, others are not. One of the most important rules of the business is "Don't take chances you don't have to." There are many risks inherent to this activity and you take the ones you can't avoid without complaint. However, it is important to minimize the chances for injury whenever possible. Being injured decreases your ability to decoy. You let down the people who rely on you and the dogs also suffer. It is not a matter of courage, it is a matter of good sense and practicality. Good decoys are hard to find and trainers cannot afford the luxury of having one injured. It's not good for you; it's not good for the trainer; and it's not good for the dog, who has to put up with mediocre decoys. So do what has to be done, but don't take a chance you don't absolutely have to.

While you're at it, avoid working with decoys who have a large number of scars and seem eager to brag about them. If you don't, you will probably end up with a similar number. Remember that scars are not a sign of skill. We all have some, but you should be learning the trade from someone who only has a few, and doesn't consider them a reason for bragging. The quality of people you work with is critical. There is no safe way to work with a fool. No matter how careful you are, no matter how good your equipment is, a fool will find a way to get you hurt. Don't work with them.

There are a few safety items that most decoys can agree on (see Text Box 7.1). The first was introduced above – a mind set that emphasizes safety. Try to develop "what if" thinking. Examine each situation before you get into it and make a mental list of all the things that could possibly go wrong. Make sure you have a reaction in mind for each possibility. Murphy's Law says that whatever can go wrong, will – but Murphy's Law of Decoying says that the worst possible thing will always happen at the worst possible moment. Be ready for that at all times and you have a chance for a long and productive career. Throw caution to the wind or show off for the boys or girls and you are headed for a painful, short, but exciting year or so of decoying.

Your equipment is important to safety as well. Most of the tools designed for decoying are designed to provide some measure of safety. There are too many devices on the market now to list them all, but we will try to discuss some of the common tools and their use. Note that none of them keep you safe by themselves, each can be used well or misused. It's how you use them that counts.

Stake Line

When I first began decoying, it was customary for the handler to hold the end of the dog's leash while the decoy worked. The trick was to get the handler to stay still. Often the dog would lunge at the decoy, pulling the handler off balance. The handler would then fall forward a step or two and the dog would be able to make contact at a time when

Figure 7.1

it shouldn't be able to. This got a lot of decoys bitten. At some point, trainers began "staking" the dogs, which meant that instead of being held by a human, the dog was tied in some manner to a stake or other immovable object while the decoy worked (see figure 7.1).

This was a major improvement in safety. There was no human holding the line so the decoy knew exactly how far the dog could come in his direction. As long as the dog had good drives and the decoy drew the dog out slowly to the end of the stake line before working in earnest (so it wouldn't run forward with a slack line and hit the end of it with a bang) it was quite functional and allowed the decoy to work more safely and to play tug of war more effectively (he could pull against the stake line). It also eliminated some problems caused by miscommunication with the handler. No matter what happened he knew exactly where he was safe and where the dog could reach him. The longer the stake line the more complications there are, naturally. The dog can get tangled up more easily and the decoy can misjudge the length of the line occasionally. But even with its weaknesses, it is still safer for the decoy than the old method.

Condition of Equipment

The collars, leashes and lines used to restrain the dog are the source of many problems. Collars fray and split, buckles separate, snaps break, leashes split, rivets fail – you name it and it can happen. Check these items before you work a dog and don't trust someone else to do it unless you have to. Handlers often do not appreciate the importance of decoy safety, and you should watch out for yourself whenever possible. The condition of your protective sleeves and other equipment should also be constantly monitored. A good principle to keep in mind is that anything made by man can, and will malfunction at some point. Equipment failure is a common cause of decoy injury and you should constantly be on guard against it. This is one of the major "what if" categories mentioned earlier.

Footwear

Many people disregard shoes when they think of safety items but they are important to the decoy. It is difficult to decoy well or even remain safe if you slip and fall down at the wrong times. Foot movement is a large part of the business and you need to have sure footing to do it safely. Make sure your shoes are in good repair and appropriate for the environment you are working in. For instance, cleated soccer or football shoes are best for grass field environments, but most are useless inside a building, where basketball or tennis shoes are an advantage. Good decoys often bring more than one type of footwear to work.

Bite Pants

Protective trousers, often referred to as bite pants are also important. Dogs are much faster than humans and usually have the advantage of acting first in a bite situation. If they elect to bite at a location on our body other than where we have tried to focus them, they have the advantage of reaction time and better overall speed. They will usually make contact before we can get out of the way. If they can't, they are not very good athletes. Adding to this the fact that some dogs like to bite legs more than anything else; and that many dogs take cheap bites as they come off the sleeve and at other times during control work; and that during realistic scenarios your legs are sometimes the only part of your body the dog can reach; it should come as no surprise that your legs get bitten from time to time.

Another factor in favor of using bite pants is that proper sleeve presentation requires the decoy to stand up and force the dog come up to the sleeve in order to bite. This technique is a result of problems reported some years ago where dogs trained by decoys not using bite pants failed to bite fleeing felons because the criminals did not bend down to present the sleeve. Old style decoys always bent down when the dog was about to bite because it was the only reliable way to keep the dogs from biting their legs. Some dogs apparently learned that if a bite was required in a situation, the decoy would be bending down to present the sleeve. They began to read this as a cue for when to bite and when not to. When the real criminals ran off down the street they did not slow up and bend down, so the dogs didn't bite them. Some actually ran alongside the felon, looking right at him, as if they were wondering when he would slow up and bend down with the sleeve. They didn't bend and the dogs never bit them, allowing some to escape completely, much to the embarrassment of the K-9 units.

So now we try to stand up as much as possible, making the dog come up higher to get the bite. It seems to be helping the situation. However, without bite pants it is hard for the decoy to stand up straight knowing there is a good chance the dog will bite his unprotected legs. So wearing bite pants has helped decoys stand up better, knowing that their legs are covered to some extent. This in turn has directly helped the dogs.

Miscellaneous Items

Several other items could be mentioned, such as groin protectors (which no one appreciates until they take a groin bite) and hand covers for use with hidden sleeves, etc. They all have strengths and weaknesses and are usually a matter of style and personal choice.

Good Handler

One last item should be emphasized before we move on, though. A good handler is probably the best piece of safety equipment available. When things go wrong, there is nothing better to have around than a competent handler who wants you to come out uninjured. Decoys are frequently saved by the skill of a good handler. As stated earlier, there is no safe way to work with a fool. They will not only get you into trouble, they are often no good at getting you out.

Starting Without Dogs

There are several skills necessary for decoy work that are best taught without a dog. Regardless of your decoying philosophy, there are steps in developing new decoys. Perhaps the most important thing is what to avoid. What you don't do is what was done to most of us – put a sleeve on someone, tell them to go out on the field to start taking bites, and try to "coach" them through it. All that does is guarantee a maximum number of mistakes which will affect the dogs negatively and a maximum level of confusion or frustration for the decoys who are being asked to do things they are not ready for. So let us examine some elementary drills which can help prepare the new decoy to meet his first dog. There is probably more than one way to accomplish this, so don't feel that you have to do exactly what you read here. Feel free to start with these drills though, since

---

Text Box 7.2

Drills Without Dogs

1. **Flag drills for footwork and timing**
2. **Sleeve locking drills for proper presentation**
3. **Tape drills for bit placement**
4. **Sleeve line drills for balance and figure 8 motions**
5. **Stick drills with sleeve line**

they have worked well for several years in my decoy schools and workshops (see Text Box 7.2).

Drills for Footwork

The best place to start working on a new decoy seems to be his feet. Most of the time a decoy doesn't need to be thinking about his footwork. He has a lot of other things to worry about and needs his feet to take care of themselves. When he is stimulating territorial aggression or doing civil agitation (working the dog with no protective equipment) he needs to be able to jump in and out of the dog's space or territory when he wishes with such good timing that he does not get bitten.

To develop this kind of footwork, you can play a game of flags. Divide your students into pairs, with one playing the dog's role and the other being the decoy. They can switch roles from time to time so each gets an equal amount of work in both. Place some type of flag or cloth strip in the belt of the decoy, one on each hip. Connect the student playing the part of the dog to a stake line (usually we tie it around the waist), and have him get down on his hands and knees to imitate the position of a dog (see figure 7.2). Mark the semicircle which describes how far out he can reach towards the decoy and then a second semicircle just inside that curve. The drill is then to have the decoy approach the

Figure 7.2

student playing the role of the dog, and touch the inner semicircle with one of his feet while moving laterally in front of the student playing the role of the dog. The trick is to do this without the "dog" being able to

Figure 7.3

Figure 7.4

grab one of the flags. This requires good footwork, speed and timing (see figure 7.3).

We repeat this drill several times in my decoy schools and to create some motivation I usually add the following rule: at the end of each pass, one of the two students does three pushups. If the "dog" has a flag in his hand, the decoy does the pushups. If the "dog" has no flag in his hands and the decoy touched the inner circle with his foot, the "dog" does the pushups. If the decoy fails to touch the inner semicircle with his foot, naturally he does the pushups regardless of the outcome (see figure 7.4). After several repetitions, students are eager to avoid the pushups (anyone who is not healthy enough to safely do three pushups

Figure 7.5

should not be in decoy training. If there is an exception to this, you can adjust the penalty accordingly). The decoys are also eager to improve their footwork. Add to this drills where the decoy is supposed to pick a straight line to run which will intersect with and actually allow the "dog" to take a flag (see figure 7.5), and you have taught approach angles as well.

Sleeve Presentation and Bite Placement

The next thing to work on is sleeve presentation and bite placement. Still working in human pairs as described above, the decoy is

Figure 7.6

fitted with an external sleeve and required to hold it in front of him with the thumb of the sleeve hand held as tightly as possible to his navel and the outer sharp edge of the same hand facing out and slightly down towards the dog's mouth (see figure 7.6). He is then required to hold the sleeve still while running approach patterns in front of the "dog." When he can do this properly, he can begin to move his sleeve arm naturally, providing he can lock it into position whenever the instructor calls for it.

Figure 7.7

Then the "dog" is given some form of sticky tape, such as masking tape, rolled up into a ball with the sticky portion on the outside. As the decoy passes in from of him, the "dog" lunges straight forward and pushes the tape straight forward onto the sleeve (see figure 7.7). This approximates (somewhat roughly) the location on the sleeve where the dog would have bitten. The decoy is then required to move the sleeve arm during the passes in such a fashion as to place the tape in a particular spot on the sleeve without making motions which will jam the dog in the mouth later. It doesn't hurt at this point to have the decoy hold the sleeve a few inches away from the body and pull it back in when the "dog" hits the sleeve with the tape. This encourages catching the dog by absorbing some of the shock rather than jamming the dog in the mouth. Placement of the tape on the wrist, in the middle of the forearm and near the elbow should be possible whenever the instructor calls for it (see figures 7.8 and 7.9). It is vitally important to have each student do these drills with both arms, unless physical problems prevent it. A decoy who can place bites on either arm is much more valuable than one who can only do it on one side.

Figure 7.8

Figure 7.9

How rough an approximation this is of where the dog will bite is not the issue. The purpose of this drill is to introduce the idea of bite placement and show the decoy that things can be done to affect it without jamming the dog in the mouth. This drill has been very successful in teaching the movements and ideas needed for this. Purely for amusement we sometimes add the pushup rule to the placement of the tape, although the "dogs" tend to cheat which makes it quite difficult for the decoys.

Working the Sleeve

Working the dog on the sleeve is the next step. Still working in human pairs, the sleeve is fitted with a small rope or leash so that the "dog" can grab it and pull on the sleeve (see figure 7.10). The dog stops

the decoy by taking hold of the sleeve leash and pulling him forward and from side to side (see figure 7.11). While the "dog" is doing this, the decoy is required to work the sleeve slowly and gently by moving the wrist in small figure 8 motions (see figure 7.12). This teaches the decoy to keep on balance with the dog tugging in different directions and to work the dog in a safe manner.

Figure 7.10

Figure 7.11

Figure 7.12

Other patterns of sleeve motion can be introduced later, but the figure 8 motion is safe for the dog and simple for beginners to learn.

Before the acceptance of hard sleeves, bite bars and the like, decoys used to do some pretty wild things with the dogs on their sleeves. We used to thrash the dog up and down, picking them right off the ground and then spinning around, swinging the dog (who was still biting the sleeve) through the air. Eventually we began to realize that some dogs were sustaining neck injuries from these activities and others were snapping canine teeth and absorbing other oral damage. So we started to get more conservative in our decoying styles. Part of the problem was that years ago we trained more dogs with less natural aggression than we would have liked. They needed more stimulation when on the sleeve to give us the amount of fight we wanted from them. Consequently we developed the habit of working in a wild, stimulating manner to keep them at an acceptable level of aggression. We were also using softer sleeves routinely. There was much less chance of tooth damage with such equipment. When we got better at selecting dogs with higher levels of aggression, we needed harder sleeves to protect our arms, but had the habits of soft sleeved decoys. This created some problems until we learned to adjust to dogs that didn't need as much stimulation and could actually hurt themselves on hard sleeves.

Anyway, the idea now is to select dogs with natural forms of aggression, catch them well and work with conservative, small and slow movements when they are on the sleeve (even if you are using a soft sleeve). The figure 8 motion seems to be the most preferred pattern at this time.

Stick Work

Figure 7.13

If stick work will be required of the decoy, or if you simply want to train all your students for it just in case they have to do it some day, this would be a reasonable time to introduce it. It can be done with the sleeve leash or line tied to something solid in the manner of a stake line. With the stick in the non sleeve hand, the decoy can practice hitting the line, which should be stretched tight (see figure 7.13). This should be kept up until able to make full striking motions with good speed, coming within a half an inch of the line, but not touching it. Then the decoy should run around the semicircle doing it. When proficient at this, small balloons can be taped to the line. Decoys can then practice striking them without bursting them.

When proficient at these types of drills, the decoy is better prepared to meet the first dog. He has some idea of how to judge distance and speed approaching a dog; which angles to use when doing so; how to absorb some of the shock of impact; how to place a bite where it is wanted on the sleeve; how to avoid jamming the dog in the mouth; and how to stay standing up and work the dog after it makes contact. All this without having the slightest chance of hurting a dog. This produces a much higher probability of success with the first encounter with the dog, thus building confidence and allowing enjoyment of the work. This will also be appreciated by the dogs.

8

Common Procedures

It is beyond the scope of this book to list all the possible procedures that decoys use in the course of their careers. It is more practical to describe some of the more common procedures. This will provide a uniform starting point and more advanced procedures can be added at a later time under the direct supervision of a competent instructor. By practicing these procedures enough of the basics will be learned to be useful to any trainer, which makes it easier for further modification to personal style and needs.

Civil Agitation

Civil agitation is a term used for work done with the dog on a stake line or held by a handler, and the decoy with no protective equipment. The goal is to stimulate the dog to try to bite the decoy when the decoy is dressed normally, but not to actually let it happen. The decoy uses whatever body signals are necessary to trigger the type of aggression the trainer wants to work with, and uses a lot of fancy footwork (like the flag drill in the previous chapter) to tantalize the dog and get back out of the way before it makes contact. Civil agitation can be used at different stages in a dog's training, but is always risky for the decoy. This is one of the risks that needs to be taken but be sure everything else is working, ensuring safety.

Sack or Tug Work

Other procedures are specifically designed to encourage contact between the decoy and the dog. New or young dogs are often started with "sack work." This is a phase where the decoy stimulates whatever form of aggression is appropriate in the dog (see chapters 4, 5 and 6 for a discussion of this) and builds the frustration to a pitch. When the trainer feels that the time is right for the dog to actually bite something the decoy presents a rolled up burlap sack, other rolled up fabric or a tug toy. The sack is carried for several sessions before the bite actually takes place. The decoy focusses the dog on the sack by repeatedly dangling it within reach of the dog and then pulling it back out of reach just before the dog can catch it. It is important to move the sack towards the dog slowly and pull it back fast, not the reverse. Merely hitting the dog in the face with the sack does not work well in many cases. By moving the sack more than anything else the decoy can get the dog to pay so much attention to it that the dog hardly notices anything else. During this time the decoy uses the appropriate body signals to trigger whatever type of aggression the trainer wants to work with. Presentation is often made at the end of a pass as the decoy switches direction.

Figure 8.1

Figure 8.2

Figure 8.3

The sack should be held in the hand nearest the dog and as the decoy turns toward the dog to change direction, the sack is swung firmly into the dog's mouth, placing it as far back as possible (see figures 8.1, 8.2 and 8.3). When the dog bites it the decoy acts appropriately depending on which type of aggression the trainer is trying to develop. If predatory aggression is the object, the decoy would play a momentary game of tug of war, letting the dog rip the sack out of his or her hand, continuing to use distance decreasing signals and run off.

A major variation of this procedure, for dogs who only have predatory aggression, and rather low levels of that, is to tie the sack onto the end of a leash or line. The decoy then drags it behind like a trolling fisherman. This decreases pressure by increasing the distance between the dog and decoy and strongly imitates the height and movement of prey animals. The dog is held on leash by the handler and allowed to chase after the sack in a straight line pursuit (see figure 8.4). When the trainer decides it is time for the dog to bite, the decoy runs slow enough to let the dog make contact. The brief tug of war can be conducted using the line so the decoy never has to come close to the dog (see figure 8.5).

Figure 8.4

Figure 8.5

Gradually the distance is decreased between the decoy and dog until the dog is doing normal predatory aggression work. Getting back to the normal type of sack presentation, if the trainer is trying to use social aggression, the decoy would alternate distance increasing and decreasing signals while playing tug of war (see figure 8.6 and 8.7), finally admitting defeat, dropping the sack and running away.

Figure 8.6

Figure 8.7

If the trainer is trying to use the fear induced aggression, the decoy would use as many severe distance increasing signals as the dog could tolerate while playing tug of war (see figure 8.8), finally dropping the sack and running off. Whatever type of aggression is being used, sack placement and tug of war are important. Putting the sack in the back of the mouth teaches a dog that it has more power when using the entire mouth (this encourages a full mouth bite). Tug of war is used to develop the dog's jaw muscles, much as exercise strengthens any other set of muscles. It is amazing how hard a dog can bite after a good program of tug of war.

Figure 8.8

External Sleeves

The new dog often graduates to soft external sleeves next. Sometimes the sack must be tied around the sleeve to bridge the mental gap, but many times the dog will bite a sleeve the first time it sees one (particularly if a dog with strong aggressive tendencies is selected). Harder sleeves can be introduced next to protect the decoy. External sleeve work is merely an extension of the drills described in chapter 7. The decoy uses the same angles of approach, sleeve presentation, bite placement, balance and figure 8 sleeve motion as in the drills with no dogs. It will help some dogs if they are focussed on the sleeve the same way as being focussed on the sack. If the sleeve is the object which is placed within reach, only to be removed just before the dog can get it, the dog will pay attention to little else until it can get the prize.

Much of this game is played with the feet, moving close enough for a bite and then jumping back just in time to prevent it. Making the sleeve the most interesting object around helps some dogs tremendously. Once the dog is focussed, the decoy can present the sleeve and allow the bite to occur. Then be sure to slowly draw the dog out to the end of the stake line before working hard (to avoid having the dog bang into the end of the line), and to change direction just before presenting the sleeve (see figure 8.10). This change of direction places the dog slightly behind the motion of the decoy, making it easier to get a good bite. It is often referred to as "cocking the dog."

Figure 8.9   Figure 8.10   Figure 8.11

Once the dog is on the sleeve, the decoy should step gently backwards as far as necessary to keep the line snug or as close to it as the dog can handle (see figures 8.9, 8.10, 8.11 and 8.12).

This way if something goes wrong, safety is within one step. Some trainers like to start the bark and hold procedure at this stage, where the dog must learn to sit and bark if the decoy is not moving. Not all trainers do this, but the ones that do like to neutralize the dog before they go too far in its training. They have the decoy walk up and stand motionless directly in front of the dog. When the dog sits and barks, the decoy rewards it by moving to the side and presenting the sleeve just as in the final stage of the other approaches, allowing the dog to bite.

The dog eventually learns to sit and bark if the decoy is motionless in order to get the bite. When the dog is good at this, the dog is said to be "neutralized (see figure 8.12b)."

Figure 8.12a   Figure 8.12b

The major addition to this phase of decoying is that some dogs with lower levels of aggression need help holding the sleeve. One way to encourage them to stay on the sleeve is for the decoy to rotate the wrist of the sleeve arm back and forth in small motions after the dog has taken a bite. The rotations should be small but fast, producing a form of vibration in the sleeve without making it difficult to hold. This imitates the wriggling of a prey animal and encourages the dog to bite harder to hold it. As they become better at holding on, the decoy can stop vibrating the sleeve and lean back and play tug of war with the sleeve, since the dog is on the stake line and the line is tight. Fear of losing the sleeve will encourage many dogs to bite harder.

When the decoy is proficient on the stake line, short pursuits can be introduced. The distances can be increased as balance is mastered, until covering as much territory as wished.

Dropping the External Sleeve

The major addition to external sleeve work is the subject of dropping the sleeve. This is when the decoy deliberately lets go of the sleeve, allowing it to slip off the arm when running away (for this reason it is often referred to as slipping the sleeve). It is a form of reward for the dog and is used frequently with new or young dogs. Everyone agrees

Figure 8.13

that young dogs like to pull the sleeve off the decoy and enjoy running around with it in their mouths (see figure 8.13). The controversy arises when we consider how often this should be done. If it is done too much (how much this is will vary from dog to dog) it encourages the dog to become "sleeve happy," a condition where the dog knows that the object of the game is to bite the sleeve, not the man.

It is possible for sport trainers to increase a dog's scores on the competition field by deliberately focusing the dog on the sleeve. So sleeve happy dogs can be quite successful in the sport world and offer their owners limited liability since they literally will not bite a human, only sleeves. Other sport trainers want a dog that will actually protect them, and don't drop the sleeve very often at all, preferring to focus the dog on the man. So within the ranks of sport competitors, dogs that will never bite humans can be found, others that will do serious protection work, and all shades of grey in between.

Police service dogs need to be focussed on the adversary, not some piece of equipment the decoy may or may not be wearing. On the other hand, it is nice to be able to reward the dog with a sleeve drop on occasion. Fortunately there are ways to do both, but the decoy and the handler must be well coordinated with each other. There are two major approaches, each working well on different dogs. The first is to work the dog on the stake line, dropping the sleeve at one end of a pass (see figure 8.14). Instead of leaving the area, the decoy stops, waits a second, moves laterally away from the sleeve and then restimulates the dog (see figure 8.15). Many dogs will drop the sleeve immediately and move away from

Figure 8.14

Figure 8.15

Figure 8.16

it to meet the new challenge (see figure 8.16). Since the decoy has no sleeve at this point, the dog is clearly showing aggression towards the man, not the sleeve. If it is necessary to test a sport trained dog for police work, this is not a bad way to do it. If the dog spits the sleeve out five times in a row to get at the returning decoy, a good candidate is probable. If the dog doesn't, perhaps this dog is not a good candidate. Some dogs have trouble with the above method, some due to being sleeve happy, others due to a propensity for pain induced and redirected aggression. As the decoy restimulates them, they redirect their aggression into the sleeve, which is close at hand, and simply bite the sleeve harder. The more the decoy works them, they more they bite the sleeve. If the decoy hits them with a stick, they just bite harder since any aggression that is stimulated gets redirected to the sleeve. It's a no win situation. If this is what is happening, there is another approach which may work better.

When the decoy drops the sleeve and freezes, have the handler pick the dog up gently by the agitation collar (not the choke collar) until the dog's front feet are just off the ground (see figure 8.17). Wait patiently until the dog drops the sleeve. This may take a long while with some dogs, but most will eventually drop it. Choking the dog off does not teach what we wish the dog to learn, so try to avoid that if possible. When the dog releases the sleeve, have the decoy move laterally and restimulate the dog. Have the handler step laterally to follow the decoy, carrying the dog away from the sleeve, which should be on the ground. When the dog is far enough away from the sleeve, the handler puts the dog's front feet back on the ground to let it respond to the decoy (see figure 8.18).

Figure 8.17

Figure 8.18

The handler should be careful if the dog is prone to redirected aggression, since the handler is now the nearest available object. If this still doesn't work well, take the dog off the stake line, have the handler hold the dog on leash, and try another variation. When the decoy drops the sleeve, have the handler pick the dog up by the collar as before (see figure 8.19). When the dog releases the sleeve, have the handler step over it and walk forward several steps as the decoy moves away stimulating the dog (see figure 8.20). For some reason, it is easier for some dogs to make the switch this way. Whatever way is chosen, the point is to bring the dog back to the decoy when the sleeve is dropped. This teaches new dogs not to get sleeve happy even though the sleeve is dropped for them sometimes, and it helps rehabilitate dogs who are already sleeve happy (although some of them never make a complete transition).

Figure 8.19

Figure 8.20

Hidden Sleeves

Another way to minimize problems with equipment orientation is to work the dog with hidden sleeves. This requires not only the sleeves, but large amounts of loose clothing that can be thrown away when it gets ripped. The main differences between this and external sleeve work is that it hurts more and bite placement is critical since the hand is often

Figure 8.21

Figure 8.22

exposed. The best way to introduce the new decoy to hidden sleeves is to go back to the stake line with a good dog. Run your approaches the same way but make sure the bite is placed as near the elbow as possible (see figure 8.23). When the dog is on the sleeve, make sure the decoy keeps the wrist higher than the elbow (see figure 8.24).

When dogs remouth or slip, gravity brings them down the arm. If the wrist is lower than the elbow, the dog will be slipping in the direction of the exposed hand. It is safer to keep the dog high on the forearm, as far away from the hand as possible. This is why strict attention should be paid to bite placement from the very first drills decoys run, even the ones with a human partner and the tape described in a previous chapter. By the time they get to hidden sleeve work, their habits are formed and they will wish they had paid more attention to detail.

If unfamiliar dogs must be worked, a hand protector may be a wise thing to use, although dogs can tell easily what they are. Also remember that most hidden sleeves have some bulk to them. Having one sleeve on and nothing on the other arm makes it easy for the dog to tell that they have one on (even humans can see the difference). Consequently it is best to work the dog such that the hidden sleeve is on the arm away from the dog. The decoy should focus the dog on the unprotected arm by making most of arm motions with it (see figures 8.21 and 8.22). When turning toward the dog to change direction at the end of the pass, the protected arm can be slipped between the body and the dog and move in close enough to allow the dog to make contact at the same time (see figures 8.23 and 8.24). This gives the dog little time to notice any difference.

Figure 8.23

Figure 8.24

Since it was focussed on an unprotected arm, it makes the decision to bite an unprotected arm. By the time it notices the difference, the decision is past. Whether it is this deception or simply that most dogs decide that many humans wear hidden sleeves and it is alright to bite them, skillful use of hidden sleeves helps produce a good street dog.

Muzzles

Another useful tool is the muzzle. It is another chance for the decoy to work the dog without an external sleeve, although dogs can orient their behavior to the muzzle just as much as they do to external sleeves if the work is not balanced enough with other forms. But this is true of all types of decoying. One of the big advantages of muzzle work is that it allows the decoy to work the dog with no protective clothing at all. In fact, many dogs benefit from being rewarded for trying to bite a human in nothing but a bathing suit or shorts and tee shirt. When the decoy has nothing but a bathing suit on, it knows we weren't asking it to bite protective devices under the sleeves or trouser legs. It helps many of them stay focussed on the man rather than arm or leg sleeves. Agitation muzzles are different from regular muzzles, so be sure that the dog has one that allows it to breathe and bark but doesn't come off when put on properly. Also make sure that no teeth can stick through any openings as this will cause bad gashes (see figure 8.25).

Figure 8.25

Before using the muzzle in aggression work, it should be worn frequently during obedience, other assignments and down time so that the dog adjusts to it, ignores it and focusses through it mentally. If you put it on just during aggression, many dogs will spend their time trying to get the muzzle off instead of confronting the decoy.

When to start muzzle work is a controversial topic. Some trainers feel that using the muzzle requires a dog with a high level of aggression. They say that if you put a dog into this type of work without sufficient aggression levels, it will be overfaced (confronted by something it can't handle) and psychological damage will be done which is often difficult to repair. They feel that muzzle work should be put off until the dog with medium aggression levels has had time to develop higher levels. However, other trainers have reported good success using muzzles even with weak dogs. Both sides agree that dogs with naturally high levels of aggression can begin muzzle work any time the trainer feels it is appropriate. If unsure whether to start it or not, it is probably safer to delay it until you're sure.

It might be best to introduce the decoy to the muzzle after confidence has been developed. Many people find muzzle work more disturbing emotionally than other forms of decoying. If you are one of them, do not get down on yourself for being a wimp. You will get used to it with time and positive exposures. The only question is how long it will take. If you put the dog on the stake line again, at least for the first few sessions, the decoy will feel better. Decoys should make sure they are wearing thick enough clothing to absorb the pressure of the dog's toe nails, which can make nasty welts on human skin. If the decoy is supposed to have minimal clothing on, they should insist that the dog wear boots over the toe nails. They should also test each muzzle themselves. This is done by standing in front of the dog, grasping the muzzle by the sides with both hands and pulling strongly towards themselves, to see if they can pull the muzzle off the front of the dog's head (they should not twist or pinch the dog when doing this).

Figure 8.26

Figure 8.27

When all is ready, the decoy begins work normally. If the dog is confused, it helps some to put an external sleeve on for the first few sessions, until the dog realizes that it is supposed to show aggression. When the time is right for a bite, the decoy moves close enough to allow the dog to make contact, falling to the ground the instant the dog strikes him. He then uses distance decreasing signals and crawls off as though injured (see figures 8.26 and 8.27).

As the dog gets bolder, the decoy can fall at the dog's feet and let it stand over him or her (the ultimate signal of dominance and victory for the dog) (see figure 8.28).

Figure 8.28

As the dog's confidence rises, the decoy can stand up for a few seconds before falling down, extending this time until it is not necessary to fall down at all (see figure 8.29).

Figure 8.29

Using the hands too much at this point can encourage some dogs to focus on them instead of the arms and body. Consequently many good decoys try to fight the dog using their forearms and elbows when doing muzzle work, keeping their hands back and out of the way. They are careful not to strike the dog with the elbows when doing this.

Figure 8.30

Figure 8.31

Then the dog can be taken off the stake line and moving bites can be worked on in a similar manner to external sleeve work. When the short pursuits begin, it is often helpful for the decoy to fall down again as soon as the dog makes contact (see figure 8.30). It is important for the decoy to use hands to cover the eyes and ears when this is being done (see figure 8.31).

The dog usually comes back and begins biting, or trying to bite, the prostrate or crawling decoy. It is simple for the dog to rip the decoy's ears and eyes with its toe nails during this process, even though its teeth are ineffective. Remember that by lowering his height and using distance decreasing signals, the decoy will stimulate predatory aggression. In this situation, many dogs will bite and claw at the head and neck more frequently than in other circumstances.

This is natural, since the object of predatory aggression is to kill the prey animal in order to eat it. Neck and head bites do this more efficiently, so the decoy should protect that area as well as possible, even though probably getting bashed by the muzzle in all parts of the body before geting up. As before, the decoy begins to stay up for an instant before falling down, increasing the amount of time remaining standing erect according to the dog's confidence levels and willingness to fight (see figure 8.32 and 8.33). Once the dog is confident enough for the decoy to remain standing, the trainer can conduct all the drills that can be done with a regular bite sleeve, including handler protection, control work, pursuits, and drills which include the termination of pursuit before the dog makes contact with the decoy.

Figure 8.32

Figure.8.33

Muzzles can also be used to encourage the dog to bite areas of the body other than the arms. Scenarios can be invented in which the fleeing decoy leaves only his legs hanging over the top of the fence, or through the gap he is stuck in, so that the dog must bite the legs or get nothing at all. Dogs that work with good decoys and muzzles can be taught any form of body bite desired.

Bite or Body Suits

Some trainers prefer to use full body bite suits for this. Working in a bite suit is similar to the other procedures described above in that it requires the same approach angles, arm presentation, timing, etc. It requires the decoy to practice more in the beginning to master the mechanics of balance and movement (which are more difficult in a suit). Once the suit is mastered, the decoy can focus the dog on different body parts by moving them more and making them more interesting than the other parts of the body, or arranging the situation so that the only place the dog can bite is the body part you want it to bite. Decoys are often safer in suits than without them. Suits can offer big advantages in many situations.

Stick Work

Stick work can be introduced during any of the above phases of decoying, although many people are highly distracted when they first start hidden sleeve or muzzle work (they are worried about their physical safety). And when they first start wearing a bite suit, they can hardly move. So most do better if sticks and weapons are introduced after they are confident in their ability to move in a bite suit, take real bites and survive muzzle work. So while it may be done at any time, it might be wise to introduce sticks to decoys on the stake line after they are somewhat experienced. As with the drills without dogs, they can begin by using the stick on the stake line itself just behind the collar of the dog, first just stroking the line gently, then progressing to light taps and finally to stinging blows, but all on the line itself. When they have mastered that, they can work off the stake line, controlling the stick on the dog itself after it makes contact with the sleeve.

Blank Cartridges

While we are talking about weapons, a word or two about blank guns is probably in order. It seems that dogs can tell the difference in frequencies between the different calibers. It is possible to have a dog that is confident when a .38 caliber blank is fired, and yet gunshy when a .25 caliber blank is fired. Fortunately it is not common, but it happens enough to make it advisable to work your dogs on different calibers.

Blank guns are not as safe as everyone thinks, either. While it is true that no projectile comes out of the barrel, it is not true that *nothing* comes out of the barrel. Most large caliber blank cartridges have a wad to hold the powder in. These wads are shot out of an unblocked barrel when the gun discharges and are quite capable of inflicting damage. They can strike people in the face causing damage, including blindness. Dogs are not immune to this type of injury. They can break windows and knock objects off of desks and shelves. If you are dealing with shotguns, the wads are large enough to do serious damage in several ways. It is best to treat blank guns very carefully. They should not be aimed into the face of any animal (humans included) at close range and probably should not be aimed directly at any part of a human body when it is not an absolute necessity.

Even more dangerous is the practice of using blanks in real service weapons. This is good for realism, and actually required by some certification standards, but extreme caution must be used. Live ammunition at the wrong time would be deadly. Any good firearms instructor can tell you that human beings make mistakes. Documented stories abound regarding officers who have had accidental discharges with weapons they thought were empty; or rushed into dangerous situations with empty sidearms (they forgot to reload); or died trying to fire a semiautomatic with the safety still engaged; or went on duty forgetting to replace the blanks used in training with live rounds. It is unreasonable to assume that you will not make a mistake. Everyone makes them.

The trick is to develop habits which have the gun in a safe condition when you make your mistake. So if you cannot obtain or make weapons with blocked barrels (the best alternative) at least have a rule that two separate people check the condition of every service weapon and its ammunition before it is used. Also avoid aiming it directly at dogs or humans. "Someday," when you make your mistake, you will be glad you operate that way. Probability says that someday someone is going to shoot someone accidentally. Make sure that it is someone else, not you. Two separate people should also check every service weapon and it's ammunition before it is returned to duty.

Whips

There has been a lot of interest in whips lately. They can be used in many different ways, but the best is for auditory stimulation. The sound of a whip has a definite effect on some dogs, stimulating them to higher levels of aggression. Sled dog drivers have used this effect during races for a long time, and now decoys are benefiting from it. Actually we have been using auditory stimulation for years. Many old time trainers still like to fire blank guns during decoy work, feeling that it makes the dogs more aggressive. This is true, but was the source of many tactical problems until we learned to train dogs for a neutral reaction to gunfire. Anyway, this reaction to sound is the same thing that stimulates dogs when the whip is used correctly. Naturally this means that we can create the same problem of having dogs show aggression every time they hear something that sounds like a whip if we don't balance its use properly. A whip can be used to inflict pain on a dog, but that is not its best use. Small amounts of pain are best applied with other items and hitting dogs with whips is a public relations disaster looking for a place to happen. Be careful. Better yet, be wise.

A decoy who has mastered the common procedures and tools described in this chapter should be able to adjust to other procedures as trainers work with them. The decoy should not be hurting dogs by making basic mistakes and should be useful in the production of police service dogs as experience is gained. If you can work your way through this book under the tutelage of a good trainer and decoy, you will have a good start in one of the most fascinating phases of police dog training. Good luck.

Index